From There to Here
Points on the Circle of Life

The printing of this book was made possible
by a generous contribution from Elaine Strauss
in memory of her husband, Murray Kaplan

From There to Here
Points on the Circle of Life

JRC Press • Evanston, Illinois

Editors: Mel Patrell Furman, Carol Kanter, Adrienne Lieberman, and Lynn Pollack
Project Coordinator: Elaine Strauss
Designer & Producer: Darlene Grossman

Published by JRC Press, 303 Dodge Avenue, Evanston, IL 60202-3252
847.328.7678
fax 847.328.2298
www.jrc-evanston.org

ISBN: 0-967-64154-3

Printed in the United States of America

From There to Here
Points on the Circle of Life

~❧ Contents

ᴥ Foreword

by Rabbi Brant Rosen

I am often asked why, if so much of the Torah focuses on the Israelites' journey to the Promised Land, do we never actually get to read about the actual entrance itself? The final book of the Torah, *Deuteronomy,* seems to end precipitously, with the death of Moses and the new generation of Israelites standing on the threshold of entering their land. It is at this moment in the Torah reading cycle that Jewish tradition directs us to rewind back to *Genesis,* back to the very beginning. For what possible reason could we be denied this critical closure to our story?

As many have pointed out, the Torah is not a book with a conventional literary arc; i.e., a beginning, middle and end. It reads, rather, in a cyclical manner—a never-ending, ever-unfolding experience of the Israelites' journey toward a place of promise. In this way, we are meant to understand that fulfillment comes not from reaching our final destination but in charting the journey itself.

And so too for us. None of us lives in linear fashion. There are no true destinations, only those crucial moments of transition along the continuing spiral of our lives. Typically, we tend not to recognize these moments when they occur. It is usually only with the wisdom that comes with hindsight that we understand the importance, and the holiness, of such moments.

To this end, the Jewish Reconstructionist Congregation is proud to share our latest collection with you. Each entry in this volume charts a sacred moment in the cycle of an individual life. But taken together, they might also represent the collective journey of fellow travelers. The story of an individual becomes the story of a family, a community, a people. It is ultimately the story of the human race, heading together toward the places of promise that await us.

We wish you peace along your journey. ❧

 **Introduction**
by Adrienne Lieberman

Our first three children—*Is God a Cubs Fan? Pirkei Imahot: A Celebration of Our Mothers,* and *From Oy to Joy: Our Holidays Across the Years*—are still bringing us plenty of *nachas.* Sure, we could have decided to sit back on the porch with a cool drink and a fan until that familiar "Let's have one more" feeling passed.

But instead we sowed the seeds for *From There to Here: Points on the Circle of Life.* With high hopes for our next brainchild, we presented our Jewish Reconstructionist Congregation family with yet another request to dig deep and share with us the gems they mined. In the synagogue newsletter and in weekly emails, our co-congregants read this plea:

> *Let's face it; you've changed, and so have we. Since our last congregational book came out, we've watched our kids grow up, our parents decline, and a new generation crawl toward maturity. We've marveled, too, during Yom Kippur's open mike and in High Holiday personal reflections, at the changes in you.*

> *Now we want to make those passages—the bitter and the sweet—the subject of our next congregational book. The changes you write about may be personal or public, secular or religious; and we fully expect the mood to vary from sublime to saucy.*

As before, members of the JRC community entrusted us with their stories, poems, essays, and photographs, which distilled the memories of their lives, including: a young woman's poignant embrace of her hometown; the birth of a daughter and the *bris* of a son; a woman's long-postponed reunion with her birth mother and a middle-aged man's discovery of his true cinematic identity; a son's journey with his injured father and a father's year of mourning his infant son; marriages, divorces, and remarriages; the death of a friend, a twin sister, a husband, a father, a mother; the inexorable and exhilarating cycle of generations.

We editors—Mel Patrell Furman, Carol Kanter, Lynn Pollack, and I—have felt privileged to work with the fifty talented writers of these pieces and with each other. But the year-long gestation of this book could not have come to such a happy fruition without the help of our "village," including:

- Elaine Strauss, our project coordinator, who graciously hosted every meeting and tamed the inevitable chaos of such an undertaking

- Darlene Grossman, our designer and producer, who from our mismatched files and photos created this artful volume

- Rabbi Brant Rosen, who whole-heartedly encouraged this project and wrote the foreword to the book

- Congregational Presidents Carole Kaplan and Alan Saposnik, Executive Director Bryna Cytrynbaum, and the members of the JRC Board of Directors, who have consistently supported our efforts to expand the synagogue into the world of book publishing

- Syd Lieberman, storyteller, who ordered the pieces

- Mel Patrell Furman, who copyedited and proofread them

- Jeff Winter, who wrote the glossary

And now you hold our newest baby. We'd like to think what you read here will spark memories of points on your own life's circle. As that happens, we encourage you to write your own piece, tuck it into the pages of another copy of this book, and pass it on to someone you love. We wish you a memorable journey. ❧

The committee (clockwise top left): Mel, wedding day, 1981; Adrienne with Zachary, 1977; Lynn at a definite turning point, 1960 ;Carol with transitional object, 1946; Elaine, starting school, 1930; Darlene with Gabrielle, 2004

Jeff Sklansky, Pam Cytrynbaum, Leah Sklansky, October 2001

❧ My Town

by Pamela Cytrynbaum

IN JUNE 2003 MY HUSBAND, TODDLER, dog, and I reversed the Oregon
Trail, left our life in the lush, green Northwest, and headed east for my
beloved hometown of Evanston, Illinois. I had eleven months to cram
in everything I needed to gird myself for the trek back to Oregon, land
of my own private exile.

For more than seven years, I had told my long-suffering,
wonderfully patient, empathic husband that if only I were in
Evanston I would be happy, thin, content. I would have many jobs
and opportunities, and I would love them all. I would never again
worry aloud about money, nor spend it thoughtlessly. I would have
all the personal and professional satisfaction I require. I would enjoy
harmonious relationships with every member of my family. I would
never complain.

Somewhere between the Badlands of Wyoming and the Corn
Palace in South Dakota, I challenged myself to live the approaching
year as if it were to be my last. I thought of that old game show in
which giddy contestants in a grocery store had a shopping cart and
sixty seconds to grab whatever they could. Everything they snatched
across that red line would be theirs to keep.

Now I had almost a year to live the life I had said I'd always wanted,
in Evanston, with my husband and daughter, within spitting distance
of my family of origin, my *shtetl*. One year to roam the terrain of my

past, my hometown, while forging a new future. This would be no ordinary Sabbatical, but a once-in-a-lifetime chance to live at once in the past, present, and future, and to restore, refresh, revise, transform, or abandon the relationships, habits, narratives, and truths of my whole life.

All this AND to shop at People's Market.

It was spooky, a year of living like Emily in *Our Town*. I'd always longed to play that scene in which the dead Emily hovers above her life, seeing it anew. She picks the day of her twelfth birthday to watch, but she can hardly bear it: "Oh, earth, you're too wonderful for anybody to realize you. . . . Do any human beings ever realize life while they live it?—every, every minute?"

I wanted to do just that.

Our first night in town I pulled a Lot's wife and turned my back for a millisecond. Leah, then ferociously two and a half, flung herself forehead first into the sharp wooden armrest of my mother's Swedish minimalist couch. Before I could exhale, an emergency room doctor—and Mom's tennis buddy/neighbor—raced through the door and pronounced Leah concussion-free and lucky. Lucky, indeed. This was the kind of village I had longed for. It was like, add water, get a life!

And so we did. We had Shabbat dinner with *Bubbe*. Leah picked shiny red tomatoes from *Bubbe*'s garden and planted her little heart out in my mom's backyard Garden of Eden. I worked part-time, teaching and writing and learning about social issues that kept me awake at night. I spent luxurious afternoons hanging out in wonder and awe, smeared in grass stains, counting spots on ladybugs' backs with my tireless toddler. My husband and I went on dates to the symphony and took walks by the lake. I reconnected with old friends and made some treasured new ones. We did Tot Shabbats and family jammie parties at my beloved childhood synagogue. I was even co-chair of the food committee for the Purim carnival.

For the record, there were times I tore out my hair trying to find child care because the members of my support team betrayed and abandoned me in the worst possible way: to play tennis, or leave town, or work.

And relations with parents occasionally grew undignified. FYI, Mom, I ain't trimmin' the ends of my hair. Ever. And yes, that's

Bryna Cytrynbaum and granddaughter Leah Sklansky, February 2002

what I'm wearing. And Dad, if you tell me to "relax" one more time, I will spontaneously combust, burning an enormous hole in your sanctimonious black leather home-office therapy couch.

So there were issues. But it was still worth every millisecond. Here's what I know now: You can go home again. But sometimes the oasis of home is like a drink for an alcoholic: "One is too many. A thousand's not enough."

Of course, I had wanted it all to remain the same, so when I returned I would know who I was. Like my daughter, who in those early nights after our move, when she wasn't quite asleep, whispered, "Mommy, I want to be in our house in Oregon." Funny how Oregon was her Evanston. One mom at Leah's school confided to me that Baltimore was her Evanston, and Evanston was her Oregon.

But this place is different. I am different. When I lived in Chicago as a single gal, I worked seventy hours a week and spent the rest of the time complaining about how I had no time to do anything. I always meant to have Shabbat dinner each week with my mom. I meant to go to blues clubs and Ravinia. I meant to walk by the lake to clear my head. I meant to clear my head. I meant to go to the Botanical Garden and the zoo; to take Yoga; to learn Spanish; to get married, to have children. But who had time?

I may be slow, but I'm not an idiot. This time around I made time for the ephemeral gift that God and my husband gave me, and that I gratefully, graciously, mindfully, and realistically received. You know. Pretty much.

If you had one year in the place your heart calls home, how would you live? How will you live?

Try it. Live this year like it's your last in a place you adore, a place you call home, with the people who mean everything to you. Treat yourself, your work, your family, your hometown, our home planet, like something precious you are certain to lose. ∾

Birth

by Bop* Kanter

YEH, SURE, CHILDBIRTH; THAT WAS painful. More for my wife than me, really, though our Lamaze course seemed intent on convincing me that the mother was pretty much superfluous. We huffed and we puffed, nearly blew the house down. When it was time, I remember being nudged by the fat lady sleeping next to me, who said gently, "Let's go to the hospital." I leapt from bed proclaiming, "You mean, I'm on?"

Bittersweet Street to Michael Reese. I time contractions: the "ooh-ooohs," the "ah-aahs," and the somewhat louders. I am steadfast throughout, assure my wife that her pain's my pain. Then, when the good stuff's about to happen, the birth, she's rolled out and I'm ushered down to the waiting room. Hospital rule in 1970: no husbands in the delivery room. Out in the waiting room, I decide not to smoke. Why start now?

Jodi's born. Not a boy. So much for playing catch. Sexism's the norm, so I can think that. Now they arrest you for such a thought. She's cute, but just a baby after all. Lamaze did nothing to stimulate my maternal instincts.

Fast forward a couple years. This time, from Evanston, the commute to Michael Reese is longer. Still the mystery, boy or girl,

*Bop is the nom d'plume for Arnie Kanter, bestowed by Zoe.

Zoe and Bop, May 2005

'cause nobody's figured out yet how to tell in advance. I'm pretty sure it's a boy this time. Law of averages, innumeracy. And the rules have changed; it's 1972, and husbands are allowed in the delivery room. Yippee. I pretend this is good news.

Long labor. Much puffing. Much timing. Doctor finally says the baby's sideways, not going to come out the right way. They try to coax it to shift. In the first sign of a pattern that's to continue at least through the first thirty-two years, there's no moving the kid. So it'll be a Caesarean. Husband's not allowed in. "But, but . . ." I argue. Doctor says it's like watching a gallbladder operation. I ask whether I can watch if I promise to send the gallbladder to college. Guy's got no sense of humor. No dice. My wife's disappointed. I'm not, though I don't say so. Can't say as how I've ever been much for gallbladders, or blood.

Wendy. Not a boy again. Definitely a baby. Not nearly as interesting as her two-plus verbal sister. I'm still not exactly maternal, I guess.

Fast forward a year or two. Okay, maybe twenty-nine, and I'm ready for another baby. Wendy's. I ask her when we find out what sex our granddaughter is going to be. We only do girls in our family. And why would anybody want anything else? The Chinese have it all backwards. Sure enough, our granddaughter's going to be a girl.

It's a longer trip to the hospital than from Evanston to Michael Reese. This time it's Evanston to Atlanta. We're called when contractions start, and nearly beat Wendy and Chris to the hospital. We're in plenty of time for the birth. In fact, about thirty hours in time.

Zoe. Childbirth may not be painless, but grandchild birth sure is. At last I feel maternal.

And two years later, another girl . . . of course. Phoebe Rachel. Little PR, I call her.

I can't really write about Zoe and Little PR. Some of you may not be grandparents and you'd think I was an utter loon. But wait, you'll see. There's no transition like it. Trust me. ❧

Elaine Rae Eisenstein, 1927

❧ Naming

by Elaine Rae Eisenstein Strauss Kaplan

MY MOTHER WAS FORTY-ONE YEARS old when she got pregnant with me, although she knew neither that it was me nor that she was pregnant. She went to the doctor, finally, because her stomach was fluttering a lot and she thought she might have something serious. She got the news that she was six months pregnant and I got my first name, Tumor *Eppes, eppes* being the Yiddish word for "maybe."

I often wondered why my mother had no idea that she was pregnant with me. After all, I was not her first child. My sister Sarah, who was the reason my parents married, had that honor. Sarah died when she was only nine months old. After that, no one in my family got the name Sarah; it was considered a bad luck charm. Then came two brothers, Milton and Isadore. My father changed Isadore's name to Irving, maybe because it was the more modern version, or maybe because my father simply liked it better. Milt and Irv were born two years apart and were followed two years later by my sister Pearl, the gem of the family. Five years later, Norman arrived, and two years after that came Averon. Most of my siblings' names seem pretty ordinary, but Averon—the name Abraham was called before he got holy—always seemed special to me.

Once I overheard my mother say to a friend that she had never wanted any more children after Averon was born. Instead, after focusing for so many years on raising six children, she had wanted to get on with her own active life. And, for almost eight years, she did. My mother was already one of the first women to drive a car in the city of Chicago; a long-distance swimmer who traversed the Lake Michigan shoreline at a speed of one mile an hour; a member of the Polar Bear Club; and a golfer at a time when few women played the game. Hadassah also depended on her energy as a fundraiser, so she really couldn't be bothered with another child.

Everyone knew that when my mother made up her mind to do something, it was a done deal. So, after Averon was born, she got herself all nicely stitched back together again. As far as she was concerned, that took care of that. However, this all happened a long time ago, and the only birth control she knew was to keep nursing a child or have my father sleep under the bed. Averon was eight by this time, and my father proved uncooperative. The outcome was predictable: me.

My mother tried everything she could think of, from lots of exercise to nasty-tasting things, to end her unwanted pregnancy. Nothing worked. It didn't help when my father told her that he had hoped for the pregnancy because he wanted another daughter. I don't think it helped either when the twelve-pound bundle that was me dropped into, or rather out of, her lap. At least she didn't name me Sarah.

What my mother and father named me, according to my birth certificate, was Helen Rose, a lovely name. I found out about it in my thirties when I went to get my first passport. Long before that discovery, my father changed his mind about a child's name again, and I became Elaine Rae. I was named in memory of my maternal great-grandmother and also was given her Jewish name, Yasni Rachel.

From the very beginning and at the end, his end, I was my father's favorite. Eighteen years after my mother's death, I wrote a story about all the names in my family, That was when I recognized that once I had been named so many times, so generously, so beautifully—once I had become ME—I had never been the generic, unknown child that my mother didn't want. ❧

❧ *Brit*s I Have Known

by Elliot Zashin

THE PROSPECT OF A *BRIS* IS OFTEN fraught with anxiety. In fact, circumcision has probably been a problematic ritual throughout Jewish history. The *Chumash* gives an account of the brutal slaying of the males of Shechem. These men were still recovering from their circumcisions, an expiation demanded by Jacob's sons for the rape of their sister Dinah.

In more recent history, circumcision has often put Jewish males at risk when they were the targets of Jew-haters. Yet the ancient ritual has persisted. Today most Jewish parents, both the observant and the unaffiliated, still honor this practice when they have a son.

I was seven when my only male cousin who had a *bris* was born. I did not attend, probably because my parents did not think it appropriate for me to do so. Thus my first experience of circumcision (not counting my own) did not occur until I was married and soon to be a father. I was living in Austin, Texas, where Jews were a small minority. A university colleague invited me and my wife to his son's *bris,* mostly because I was one of his few Jewish colleagues.

Although he resembled a young prophet with his long beard and intense eyes, I was not aware that he was especially observant. His field was modern philosophy, and he probably was the most overtly radical member of the faculty. So I was not prepared for his very Jewish-looking parents and the Orthodox *mohel* they had brought with them from upstate New York to perform the ritual. The young professor's nervousness was evident early in the proceedings, and when the *mohel* drew a small bead of crimson blood from his baby's penis, he blanched and his knees began to buckle. People rushed up to support him, the *mohel* tried to reassure him, and he regained his composure. I recall thinking that I surely wouldn't want to do a *bris* in this fashion.

So I consulted the Hillel rabbi at the university, who was Reform by background and progressive by inclination. He told me that if we had a son, he would officiate at the office of a sympathetic obstetrician/gynecologist, who could perform the surgery. This removed much of my apprehension about both the circumcision itself and the need for a *mohel*. There probably wasn't a *mohel* within hundreds of miles, and I doubt that my parents would have jumped at the idea of flying one in from Tucson, Arizona, where they were living.

When our first son arrived, we followed the Hillel rabbi's lead. With only a few relatives present, a brief explanation primarily for the benefit of the non-Jewish grandparents, and the recitation of a few *brachot*, we celebrated my son's induction into the Jewish people.

Four years later, living in upstate New York and expecting our second son, we faced the prospect of another *bris*. I sought out the Hillel rabbi on campus, whom I had never met, anticipating that he would be as willing to help me as the earlier one had been. So I was shaken when he told me that if I wanted a *bris* for my son, I would have to hire a *mohel* from Rochester or Buffalo. I told him that I was not Orthodox and would prefer a ceremony more like the one his colleague in Austin had arranged. He was not sympathetic, and he suggested no alternatives. Perhaps he saw me as one of the secularized and assimilated young Jews who wanted their Judaism "lite." In any case, his attitude punctured my faith in Hillel as a Jewish life preserver.

I wanted my son to be inducted into the Jewish people in a way that fit my own, admittedly tenuous, appropriation of Judaism. It never occurred to me to turn to anyone else for help, perhaps because I was preoccupied with teaching and with adapting to life in a new place where we knew few people. My father, who was knowledgeable about

Elliot Zashin, third from right, and his son Gabriel, 1971

Judaism, had become rather anti-ritual, and I had lost touch with my former Hillel rabbi. I needed to resolve this dilemma myself.

I turned to the *Encyclopedia Judaica* at the university library and began reading the entry on "bris." I was immediately struck by one sentence: "It is the father's obligation to see that his son is circumcised." That was, I decided, more important than who performed the circumcision, how many days had elapsed since birth, and who actually recited the *brachot*.

So now I had my solution: The doctor who delivered my second son would do the circumcision before my wife took our baby home from the hospital; in fact, this seemed to be routine practice at most hospitals. I found out when he was doing the surgery and, a bit embarrassed to explain why, asked if I could be there. He readily agreed, and on a cold February morning I drove up to the hospital with a *kippah* and a photocopy of the encyclopedia entry. While he operated, I said the *brachot*. For my second son, it might not have been the most auspicious induction into the Jewish people, but I felt that I had met my obligation as a Jewish father. ❧

ᜮ Remembering Joseph
by Elliot Frolichstein-Appel

IN NOVEMBER 1999 TAMAR AND ELLIOT Frolichstein-Appel had a baby
boy who died at the age of nine days from a rare viral infection. Joseph
Reuben was buried in December. One year later, family and friends
gathered to unveil his gravestone and to reflect on the preceding year.
Sam was by then three years old, Tamar was again pregnant, and
the assembled group was reminded in the chill winter air to wash
their hands, donate blood, and cherish their children. The following
remarks by Elliot were among the readings and thoughts shared at the
unveiling.

*   *   *   *   *

In November's gusty gale
I will flop my flippy tail
and spout hot soup. I'll be a whale!
Spouting once, spouting twice,
spouting chicken soup with rice.

When Joseph entered intensive care at Children's Memorial Hospital,
there was little Tamar and I could do but be there and talk to him.
In part to lessen our creative burden, in part because of its small
size, and in part because it was a favorite of Sam's, we brought along
Maurice Sendak's Nutshell Library to read aloud. Its humor and

cadences evoked smiles from Sam and warm memories of our own childhoods. Pierre didn't care—while Spanish lullabies wafted from a nearby bedside. Alligators were all around, and balloons were bursting—as we wondered what, if anything, Baby Yoyo heard. One was Johnny—receiving his own parade of visitors as we received ours.

Our favorite was *Chicken Soup with Rice*. It was all about food. It had overtones that were both Jewish and healing. It got the biggest grins from Sam. And it had—by far—the best Carole King interpretation. It also spoke to the future. With its inexorable and delightful march through twelve months, it reminded us that the world continues, even as we remained frozen in an inexplicable twilight zone. Each evening, we would come home from the hospital and put Sam to bed, reading him a second-tier story as we reserved the best for his needier brother. In the morning we would return to the hospital, tell the staff our hopes of one day seeing a Sam and Joe's Deli serving chicken soup with rice, and read stories to our son as he fought his virus.

But the various chicken soup recipes cooked up by the doctors lacked the right magic. Sendak's Nutshell Library, imbued as it was with love from so many, remained a miniature reminder of the outside world as it sat in the corner of a hospital bed now still. The books were closed.

In January it's so nice
while slipping on the sliding ice
to sip hot chicken soup with rice.
Sipping once, sipping twice,
sipping chicken soup with rice.

After Joseph's death, the months continued their march forward. Sam remained vital and delicious. We consulted with doctors and psychologists. I changed jobs; Tamar started a second master's degree. Our friends and relatives noted the passage of time, and, in their many individual ways, let us know we remained in their hearts. The Nutshell Library remained part of Baby Yoyo's world, stored with hospital bracelets, *shiva* prayers, condolence cards. Its absence from our lives recalled his absence as winter turned to spring, then summer, then fall. We denied ourselves its joy as we were denied his joy.

About two weeks ago, we lit a candle for Joseph. Not a *yahrzeit* candle, but a birthday candle. We had asked Sam what we should do for Yoyo's birthday, and the obvious answer to him was to have cake and candles. At first it seemed a bit twisted, but it grew on us as a way to recall Yoyo's brief sojourn with us and as a way to mark the passage of time. Twelve months had passed: twelve ways to enjoy chicken soup with rice, twelve steps toward Joseph moving to a more stable place in our hearts. Jewish tradition calls for ceasing the daily recitation of kaddish at the twelfth month of mourning. For better or for worse, we find ourselves shifting our energies from mourning Joseph to remembering him.

We enjoyed his birthday cake; we savored his absence. Sam blew out the candle for his brother, just as he would have had a one-year-old been with us squirming. For a birthday present—to Joseph and to ourselves—we decided to bring the Nutshell Library out of its year-long retirement.

I told you once,
I told you twice
all seasons of the year are nice
for eating chicken soup with rice! ❧

🌊 Becoming Guatemalish

by Andra Gomberg

*Thanks to Tina and Gonzalo Escobar for
introducing me to the term "Guatemalish"*

IT IS HARD TO BELIEVE THAT JUST three and a half years ago, I adopted my daughter Maya from Guatemala. At the time, Maya was thirteen months old, and I was forty-five and single.

Some months later, Maya and I entered the *mikvah* for her conversion. I remember Rabbi Brant, Cantor Howard, and the *mikvah* lady standing by the pool while I squinted to read the prayer in Hebrew without my contacts.

In the synagogue, Maya was given her Hebrew name, Jacoba, for my father, who died when I was eleven, and I gave Guatemalan friendship bracelets to all who attended. I pledged to pass on my Jewish heritage to her and, equally importantly, to honor her culture of origin always.

Right around that time, when I returned to work from adoption leave, I had the chutzpah to hire a childcare provider who spoke almost no English. I did this in spite of the fact that my Spanish was still so basic that *hombre* for man and *hambre* for hungry sounded exactly the same to me. But I was determined that Maya would learn the language from a native speaker, and thus began a two-and-a-half-year Spanish immersion experience for both of us.

During that time, Maya also toddled around *Kallah* and developed a love for *klezmer* music and challah. She renamed JRC "Shabbat House" and claimed the space and congregation as her own.

Andra and Maya, December 2004

The day Maya turned four, she and I joined ten friends at a benefit for Marimba Oxib K'ajau, a Chicago-based marimba troupe of children of Guatemalan heritage. The director took my daughter up on stage to tell all 400 people present that it was her fourth birthday. The rest of the evening, as we dined on *tostadas Guatemaltecos* and danced, people kept coming up to wish her *feliz cumpleaños.*

Right before her fourth birthday, Maya had celebrated Rosh Hashanah with apples and honey. Shortly afterwards, she brought fruit to share with her classmates and money to plant trees in Israel in honor of *Tu B'Shevat.* Just last week, my daughter came home and proudly told me that she had been the Shabbat helper.

Soon Maya and I will be making what I hope will be the first of many trips back to Guatemala. I plan to take intensive Spanish classes there. We will also visit the school where a friend volunteers through a nonprofit organization called the Amigos Project.

Sometimes the Jewish and Guatemalan pieces of our lives have come together. Due to the volunteer work of members of our congregation, I learned about MayaWorks, an organization that imports and sells handicrafts from Guatemala and uses the proceeds to fund scholarships. I helped organize a MayaWorks presentation and sale for Los Niños de Nuestros Corazónes, our support group for families who have adopted children from Latin America.

The month before, at the preschool Hanukkah party, we ate silver dollar–sized *latkes* before streaming into Room 1 for the concert portion of the program. Preschool students, teachers, parents, and an occasional grandparent scrambled for little plastic seats. Those who hesitated had to stand, like the odd ones out in musical chairs. After a rousing rendition of the Hanukkah Hokey Pokey, the musicians started in with some of the standard repertoire from my childhood: "The *Dreidel* Song" and "Hanukkah, Oh Hanukkah." Right in front, Maya was dancing with her friends and singing along. She knew all the words. So there we were, my daughter and I, as though the preschool Hanukkah party was our preordained destiny.

For me, it was, as they say, a "moment." At that moment I realized that my daughter was beginning to forge her own Jewish identity and that I had, against all odds, become a member of this joyful community of Jewish parents.

Later on, perhaps there will be Maya's Bat Mitzvah. And possibly she will also learn to play the marimba. Both would bring a lot of *nachas* to her family. In the meantime, we continue to blend our cultures into something more and more, well, Guatemalish. Sometimes, it is hard to remember being anything else. ❧

❧ A Song for Alvin

by Rebecca Hamlin

GOD IS A TALL, HANDSOME, thirty-something Jamaican man who drives a kindergarten bus in Skokie, Illinois.

I watch my little boy, in light-up sneakers, carrying a Winnie-the-Pooh backpack, struggling up the giant steps of the school bus for the first time. I realize I am holding my breath. Alvin welcomes him into the bus and keeps up a steady stream of teasing and joking all the way to school. He learns my little boy's name. "Ari" sounds beautiful in a Jamaican lilt. Alvin learns where we live, so when I am late to the stop he pulls the bus up in front of our house and beeps the horn. I have never seen him in a bad mood.

Alvin and my child play elaborate games on the bus. My child is the doctor and Alvin is the patient. Alvin is the customer and Ari is the chef. At home, Ari makes pills out of wadded-up paper and Scotch tape to bring to Alvin the next day. He makes drawings of sandwiches for Alvin. Every day my little boy jumps off the bus laughing, already looking forward to tomorrow's ride to school.

My boys are not in kindergarten anymore. One day we are walking home from school, and Alvin passes in his bus. He stops the bus, blocking traffic in both directions. He leans out the window to have a conversation with his doctor. My child is laughing.

A Song for Alex

by Rebecca Hamlin

GOD IS A SHORT, BLUE-EYED Ukrainian man who wears an orange vest and helps children cross the street in Skokie, Illinois.

He controls his corner like a benevolent king. He strides confidently out into the busy street at rush hour. He lifts his octagonal staff, and the traffic parts. Those who believe they can defy his direction are made to submit to Alex's powerful, direct stare as they approach.

My children cross this street to enter a world I will never fully know. Inside there are procedures and protocols for everything they do. Teachers and administrators and school board members and playground supervisors monitor their every move. Outside, as they cross the street, they are shepherded by Alex's strong arm.

Alex sees us coming a block away. He is gracious and gentlemanly. He wishes me a good day, a good night, a good weekend. When we are in the street with Alex, we are in a protective bubble where nothing, not even cars, can hurt us. When I walk back, Alex stops traffic for me with the same conscientious vigor as when the children are there. It is a shockingly intimate moment, Alex and I in the street, him holding his sign and looking into my face, wishing me a good day. I walk home alone. ❧

❧ The Reader

by Janet Migdow

I DID NOT GROW UP IN AN OBSERVANT Jewish household. World War II had made unbelievers of my parents. Temple was for special occasions. Girls were not Bat Mitzvahed. We never lit Shabbat candles. I never heard of *Havdalah*. I learned the prayers late in life. I still frequently fumble.

But I have always known I was a member of the tribe, the people of the book. This is what my mother taught me: To be a Jew is to read. Maybe she taught me to be the most observant of Jews, after all.

We are the people of the book. It is my earliest memory.

I am sitting on the formica floor watching my two older sisters playing school. Actually, I am playing school, too. I just don't know what school is; I am three years old. My eldest sister Andrea is seven. She is the teacher. Her most avid pupil is my sister Laura, age five. Laura is Andrea's devoted acolyte. They will both grow up to become teachers, as will several of their daughters. But that is later, much later, and this is now.

The sunlight streaming through the window honeys the tan tile and pine walls of our classroom. I sit mostly irrelevant and ignored, a prop in their game.

Andrea has a piece of paper and is drawing something we are supposed to be paying attention to. She seems very serious about what she is drawing. The lines do not form any picture. Laura appears excited. She is awed by her elder sister, who in turn dotes on her. I am content to sit in the glow of their benign neglect.

I stare at her scribbling. Lines become letters. Words begin to form in my head. I am suffused with joy. The seemingly senseless has meaning; I am reading. My world shifts on its axis.

I have been dragging books around everywhere ever since. I read sitting and standing, walking down the street, and while eating. My mother would periodically kick me out of the house into the sunshine to play; I would take a book and climb into the neighborhood tree house to read. I read because it was magic, I was curious and thirsty, and books kept me quenched and sated. I was never lonely. I was never bored.

My mother, who thought one should never sit in a house on a beautiful day, nonetheless was a great reader herself and a great advocate of my reading. Once a week she would pile all us kids into the car, including my baby brother, and take us to the library. In the days before Barnes and Noble and Borders took over the world, we went to the library. I understand some people still occasionally pay it a visit.

On our weekly adventure we were each allowed to check out five books. I read myself straight through the children's library, culminating with the shelves of aqua-blue-bound biographies. Helen Keller and Amelia Earhart both taught me to fly. Then there was nothing left for me to read. Children were not allowed in the adult library of my 1950s hometown. I was bereft.

I see her now, my consistently soft-spoken, exceedingly polite young mother, standing at the desk of the head librarian, insisting that they give me an adult library card. I am eight, tiny for my age, mousy, freckled, wearing powder-blue prescription eyeglasses. The librarian looks from me to my mother as if wondering what species we are. Why would this seemingly sane woman be asking her to give this odd child a card to the adult library?

My mother, calm but insistent, says, "My daughter has read everything in the children's library. She needs something to read." I am terrified the librarian will say no. But she nods and hands me my key to the kingdom: shelves and shelves of unread books. Five more books a week for the rest of my life.

Bliss. I carried books home and read until my parents said, "Lights out." Then with my secreted flashlight, I continued under the covers until sleep overcame me. By the time I was sixteen, I had pretty much given up sleeping.

I look around my house now. Bookshelves are everywhere. Secretly, books procreate in the dark of night. They flow like hot lava, covering everything in their path—tables and chairs, desks, radiators, and floors. My side of the bed is a fortress. Poetry commingles with literary criticism. Prayer books kiss essays on spirituality, physics, and gardening. Political theory spills over onto traumatology, literature, and mysteries.

Pinsky's translation of *The Inferno* talks to Easy Rawlins, who perfectly understands Jane Austin, while Annie Dillard, Anne Lamott, and Heschel comment on Homer. And here in my sanctuary I pray. ✺

ᔕ He's Still My Dad to Me

by Gabriel Friedman

I REMEMBER WHEN "TRAUMATIC brain injuries" was just a section in my health textbook, and "the fall from innocence" was just an archetype studied in our ninth-grade mythology unit. That was before the accident that left my dad disabled and changed the life of each person in our family. I was only twelve years old when hospital visits became a daily occurrence and phrases like "temporal lobotomy" and "inner cranial pressure" became part of my everyday vocabulary. Yet many of the most important things have not changed.

CRASH!BOOM!BANG! I jumped off my bike and turned around. A block back, I saw a stalled black Honda Accord, its windshield shattered into a spider's web. From the metal-on-metal clash, I thought the car had hit a stop sign, but as I peddled over, I found a man stretched out in front of the fire hydrant. "You hit a person!" I called out to the driver. The man had a small gash on his right forehead. His eyes were bloodshot and unfocused, and he breathed with an ugly snoring noise. Then I noticed the man's orange undershirt, and my heart started racing. It was my Dad.

"Dad!" I cried out. "Dad! Can you hear me?" He did not respond. "Mom! Aaron! Daniel!" They were far behind my dad and me on our bike ride home; I had been ahead of my dad, a block away from our house, when the car struck him. It seemed to take forever for the ambulance to get there, each second elongated with my dad's life in peril. When the ambulance finally arrived, my dad was placed on a stretcher and loaded in, and my mom rode with him to St. Francis Hospital. My brothers and I followed in an unmarked squad car. When we arrived at the hospital, we went into the chaplain's room.

"My name's Priscilla Williams," she said. We all took a seat. My mom came into the room with the release forms that were handed to her by the doctors. Priscilla, a gentle African-American, asked us what happened.

"My dad was hit by a car," Daniel said.

"How's Dad doing?" I asked.

My mom hesitantly replied, "The doctors said when he entered surgery, his body was in very good shape." This sugar-coated answer was met with skepticism from everybody in the room.

"Does any of you have a special prayer you would like to say?" Priscilla asked empathetically. Nobody answered. The extent of the damage was starting to settle in.

Friends and family poured into the hospital. The night grew increasingly tense, and I became more impatient. I kept asking my mom when Dad would come out of surgery. Then my mom gathered Aaron, Daniel, and me around her.

"Is Dad going to live?" I asked. She repeated her earlier response: "All I know is that all the biking he has been doing over the past few years has made his body stronger. . . ."

"—Is he going to live?" I interrupted, demanding a definitive answer.

"I don't know." Our heads sank.

Finally, the neurosurgeon emerged from the metal double doors at the end of the dimly lit hallway. Everyone anxiously crowded around him. The surgeon's words were strangely impersonal.

"As you know, the impact to the patient's head caused his brain to swell, increasing the pressure in his brain. The team here performed a craniotomy to reduce the swelling. Right now, the patient is in a drug-induced coma, and the staff will continue to monitor the pressure in his head."

One Sunday afternoon, eight weeks later, Dad and I played one of our favorite games in the nearly empty cafeteria of the Rehabilitation Institute of Chicago. On the thick plastic table stood the familiar yellow-holed panel and blue supports of our shabby Connect Four set, with the red and black checkers scattered across the table. Across

Rick and Gabriel Friedman, 1995

from me, my dad was seated uncomfortably in his recumbent wheelchair. An enormous scar arched over his awkwardly tilted head and disappeared into his ruffled graying hair. At the base of his neck, a pink hole had formed where his tracheotomy had been, and contusions on his right arm marked former IV tracks.

"Dad, do you want to play Connect Four?" I asked. A hoarse mumble emerged from his dry mouth. I could tell he was not interested.

"Dad, let's play Connect Four," I said assertively as I set it up. I dropped in the first black piece. My dad put in a red piece with a little look of concentration or curiosity or doubt. I took my turn, and then my dad let go of his second piece, not even checking whether it was the right color. I dropped in a black one and then waited for him.

"Dad," I called, "it's your turn." He fell asleep.

Was this the dad I used to spend long summer evenings with, locked in fiercely contested Connect Four mini-tournaments and best-of-eleven series?

One warm evening six months later, my dad and I sat down again to play Connect Four. The object of the game is to create a line of four pieces of the same color. I had already set up the worn-out game on the patio, and as soon as my dad wheeled over to our picnic table, we began playing. This time, my dad dropped in the first piece. I followed quickly. Before I knew it, all but one column of the panel was filled up. Our individual colors bordered the empty aisle, sometimes three in a row.

"Your turn," I said expectantly. Finally, just two empty spaces remained. The black piece I dropped mixed into the spotted sea of red and black. So did his red piece. Stalemate.

From these games, I knew that life was never going to completely return to normal; however, the changes that my dad underwent from his accident do not change the love and admiration I have for him. Even if he does not walk the same way or can no longer beat me at Connect Four, he is still my dad to me. ❧

Natandome Village, Mbale, Uganda, April 2005   *(Photo by Naima Cohn)*

The Slums, Mbale, Uganda, April 2005

by Deborah Wolen

IN EARLY APRIL 2005, I VISITED A Ugandan community known as "the slums." The people of these slums lived in one-room circular mud-walled houses with thatched roofs. There was no running water, no electricity, no trash pick-up, no sewers, and no latrines. There was only rudimentary economic activity here: an occasional stall selling eggs, an eight-year-old girl selling charcoal while carrying a younger sibling on her back. Adult slum residents, many of them refugees without land to farm, sat outside at midday with nothing to do. Dozens of smiling, barefoot children, dressed in rags, leapt over trash piles and discarded plastic bags to meet us, the *muzungus* (white people). The children were delighted to greet us, "Hello! How are you? I am fine!" They competed furiously to hold our hands.

Eleven of us JRC members, including Rabbi Brant Rosen, traveled to Uganda as part of a JRC Global AIDS Task Force-American Jewish World Service Delegation to learn about HIV/AIDS and sustainable development. Accompanying me was my 16-year-old daughter, Naima. After our visit to the slums, I wondered what parts of my past had led me and Naima to rural Uganda.

I sometimes have fantasized about having a different history. In my fantasy, my parents taught me to fight for social justice and encouraged my efforts. But I was born into a real family, with a real mother and father and sister, real aunts and uncles and cousins. Into that milieu came the transformative moment that pushed me toward activism.

Cicero, Illinois, then one of the most segregated communities in the North, was my hometown. My mother, whose parents emigrated from Naples, Italy, around 1910, converted to Judaism to marry my father. There was only one other Jewish family in Cicero. My older sister and I were sent to religious school at Oak Park Temple, the Reform synagogue where my parents socialized; we celebrated holidays and lit Shabbat candles.

After my sister married her non-Jewish high school sweetheart, my parents insisted that I attend religious school through high school, and they took me to weekly *Erev Shabbat* services until I left for college. I thought I had faith. I admired our scholarly but aloof Rabbi Mervis, who used his sermons to support the civil rights movement, criticize the Viet Nam war, and review books. Mr. Yacher, my eighth-grade religious school teacher, was an inner-city teacher and Old Town folk singer. He taught us about the civil rights movement, his participation in demonstrations, and his work with impoverished minority students in substandard inner-city schools. I sang "We Shall Overcome" to Mr. Yacher's guitar, though I was not quite sure what the words meant.

On Labor Day 1966, the day before I started high school, Martin Luther King led an open housing march into Cicero. My mother's whole extended family—aunts, uncles, and cousins of all ages but especially the four who were my age—had gathered in my Aunt Jen's basement for a Labor Day party. We always gathered there to celebrate holidays and birthdays. My mother's family loved my father, and he felt more accepted by them than by his own family.

Some time after the family meal, the march began. My cousins could not resist the excitement and left for the streets to join the counter-demonstrators. My uncles carried a portable television down to the basement. The TV showed enraged citizens of Cicero carrying white power signs with swastikas, jeering and shouting at Dr. King and the civil rights marchers. I was afraid to look at the TV, fearing I would see one of my cousins, one of my closest childhood playmates, carrying a swastika sign.

The atmosphere of hate poured through the TV screen into the gray-painted basement. Suddenly, my aunts and uncles, many of whom had

Natandome Village, Mbale, Uganda, April 2005 (Photo by Naima Cohn)

helped raise me, were on their feet, yelling and screaming at the TV about how Martin Luther King would ruin their property values and take their factory jobs. Racist epithets spewed from their mouths. I felt nauseated. It was like riding the Rotor at Riverview when the floor dropped.

I thought about Rabbi Mervis and Mr. Yacher. I wanted to yell at them about books I had read, about *Animal Farm, 1984,* and Anne Frank's *Diary.* To their credit, my parents did not participate in the racist hysteria. Instead, they sat toward the back, and my mother kept telling me to be quiet or leave the room. I retorted that my mother should stand up to her brothers and sisters, tell them they were wrong. But she could not do this.

In that rarified air of adolescence, I was certain that the Jewish values of social justice that I had been taught at Oak Park Temple, though still vague and not well understood in my mind, were the only reasons I had not joined my counter-demonstrating cousins. My evaluation of my racist Cicero relatives, whom I had always viewed as appendages of myself, was harsh, without compassion, extreme. That Labor Day, I decided to cast my sympathies with those less fortunate than myself. I think that is how I ended up in rural Uganda, a *muzungu* from the richest country on earth, witnessing children's smiles in the slums of Mbale. ❧

❧ The Jade Plant

by Beth Jacoby

You arrived the same day he did
A gift swathed in cellophane,
Accompanied by balloons
And candy
Long ago consumed.
A few pillows of green
Peeked out from a blue and white bunting.
You did not stay there long.
I remember the succession of containers
Like I remember his special outfits:
The cobalt blue one
The elegant black one
The practical terracottas
Nine inches, ten inches
With matching saucers.

I also remember the day you fell and broke
Into so many pieces,
I thought nothing was salvageable.
But he insisted:
"You have to, Mom. It came with me."
And so you stand today,
With sturdy trunk and branches
Growing at an eccentric angle
(Your broken limb never set correctly).
Now, three other plants grow, too,
In different locations,
Dividends from that day.
It seems only right one should go with him
On the day he
Leaves. ❧

❧ Tell me O Muse of that ingenious hero who traveled far and wide . . .

(Homer's *Odysseus*)

by Jan Yourist

IT FIRST STRUCK ISAAC AND ME THAT something momentous was happening while on our journey to Ithaca for his theater audition for college. We were in our rental car (which we almost didn't get because I was driving on a speeding ticket I had gotten days before our trip, and New York did not believe that anyone's license was ever taken away unless there were innumerable and heinous traffic violations), driving through the remarkable upstate New York countryside, when it occurred to us that we were trying to get to Ithaca. Yes, Ithaca, just like Odysseus, the man who fought for ten years in Troy and took another ten years to get home, a journey fraught with adventures and challenges.

We already had met Polyphemos, the Cyclops, on the small plane from Chicago. He was grasping an Extreme Big Gulp soda and striking up myopic conversations with the stewardess, subjecting her and the rest of the plane for an hour and a half to the torture of his tired and trite jokes. "Did you hear that Frederick's of Hollywood is having a half-price sale?" We felt trapped like Odysseus and his men in the Cyclops' cave. (I won't bother to mention that when we ran into him while getting our rental car—his hands on the back of his car, eyes rolled up into his head screaming "Ahhh, Ahhhh"—we did not stop to ask questions.)

Isaac Francis Yourist Bloom, 2005

Landing offered escape. But finding our hotel was tricky. It was located off a roundabout, and we kept going around and around, missing our exit. Like Odysseus and his crew, who were blown off course by Aeolus' bag of winds while they were within sight of their destination, we saw our hotel fly by us again and again, so close and yet so far. And the car radio played, I know you'll never believe this, an old Cream song, "The Tale of Brave Ulysses."

"Are you listening, Mom?" Isaac smiled, filled with anticipation and an I-told-you-so expression. He had been telegraphing the message of his imminent voyage for some time now. The gods had been working on opening my ears and my heart to take it in. But the ambivalence was not only mine.

Engaging in the college process had not come easily for Isaac. He was reluctant to fill out his applications and write his essays. He was scared, anxious about what this step would bring, unsure of his ability to meet this next challenge in his life. But even the wily and crafty Odysseus was reluctant to go to Troy. He had feigned madness by plowing his fields and sowing them with salt when the Greek recruiter came.

And then, as our journey continued, we met the oracles. They were two women of epic proportions: one white, one black; one on a computer, one with a pen in hand. We discovered them behind ticket windows in a theater lobby. One looked up addresses and locations on the computer, while the other wrote down detailed longhand directions, each sharing an exhaustive critique of one play or another. Armed with their sincere but cryptic directions, Isaac and I strolled up and down the same street for over an hour and a half, fruitlessly searching for the Paul Robeson Theater. The street's name was Genesee. "Ah, we're looking for Genesis," Isaac commented as we continued our conscious odyssey.

"You're mixing your metaphors," I replied, knowing full well he was doing so on purpose. We became giddier and giddier as we somehow kept passing the address; it was an obscure location, not visible from the street, not obvious even to adventurers.

I'd like to share that on this trip we were victorious over the Laestrygonians and were enticed by Lotus Eaters, that we dodged Scylla and Charybdis, and escaped being turned into pigs. Suffice it to say, we sailed on.

On our drive to the airport, heading for home, we heard the Sirens. No, not the ones that accompany police cars and rescue vehicles, but mesmerizing voices coming from the college radio station: Dr. John's "I Walk on Gilded Splinters." Like Odysseus, lashed to the mast of his ship, I see Isaac struggling against his bonds, screaming to his crew to untie him and set him free. Unlike Odysseus' crew, I do not have wax in my ears.

So by the time we returned to Chicago, I knew that I was coming home but that the wily and crafty Isaac was getting ready to leave. Isaac's epic journey is just beginning, while I am learning to give birth for the second time. The adventure is painful and thrilling, a challenge for both of us. ❧

❧ In Transit

by Emily Rose

I creep away
on the last train
bound for anywhere
but where I've been

I look out the window
and watch the world pass by
like I'm not part of it,
like I'm on hold,
listening to bad
synthesizer renditions
of real life.

There's got to be
some destination
I just can't see
through the haze
that owns my twenties.

Every direction
equally optional
every turn a
chance for change—
No timetable,
no map to follow

I read the signs
offering products and promises
wondering if I should
join the army,
give blood,
or buy a new couch.

Searching for the toll-free number
to access the grand plan:
Press 1 for destiny
Press 2 for directions
Press 3 for personal options.

Trying to find
the express train
to where I'm headed. ➤

🌊 The First Time I Laughed

by Salli Berg-Seeley

IT HAD BEEN SO LONG THAT MY FACE actually hurt. The muscles seemed pulled into strange and unfamiliar directions, stretched almost beyond where they could go. It felt good in a painful sort of way. Like an orgasm after not having had one in years. It was true. I had barely cracked a smile since around my sophomore year in college. I was in exile. I couldn't handle the complexities of relationships with friends or lovers. I didn't even do well with acquaintances. I wish I could say that I had been affecting some sort of romantic notion of ennui, but it just wasn't that glamorous. In fact it was rather messy. I was screaming in my own skin for no discernable reason.

But at twenty-two, just after writhing through college, I got a job as a copy editor. It was the 80s; I wore navy blue designer suits bought on discount, pointy flat shoes, and faux punk spiky shag hair.

Steve always tied his own blonde-brown hair into a pony tail. His face looked unmistakably Eastern European; it was wide and smooth with green slanted eyes and a small mouth usually twisted into some exaggerated mocking expression. Steve was very slight, but he had a big butt, especially for a guy. We were sometimes mistaken for each other from behind. He looked like an androgynous teenager in black jeans and retro sunglasses. He appeared to be gay. One summer night,

Steve and Salli, c. 1990

some neighbor jerk had scrawled "Hermaphrodite" on his front door. It didn't seem to bother him.

Two weeks into my new job I was sitting in my cube, fitfully trying to unjangle someone else's jargon when Steve poked his head around and said, "Hey." We had never really spoken before, just said "hi" when we were first introduced by our supervisor, Pretty Patty. "Hey," he repeated in a friendly snarl, "Hey, do you fart a lot? I do it all the time."

He watched as my eyes widened and my jaw dropped a bit. He watched, cool and childlike, as I broke into a laugh, a real laugh—it could have been years. My stomach clenched; my cheeks ached. My face broke. I laughed. It was almost frightening. I had to grab my jaw for fear that it would become detached. This was my own certain slant of light, a wonderful, terrible crack.

Steve proved to be consistently hilarious over the years—bratty, exhilarating, even cruel, but very funny. He had the sharpest wit I've ever known, then and now. Steve was thirty going on nine. He claimed it was because he had skipped fourth grade. He was one of those whiz kids who went off to U of C at sixteen and was determined to make up for it by behaving like a brilliant idiot the rest of his life. He once compared himself to the cigar-chomping Baby Herman in the 'toon film *Roger Rabbit*. It was a pretty apt comparison.

For a few years I followed him and his Merry Pranksters around. They led me through labyrinths of galleries and bars, music venues, and a couple of drunken porch parties: barbecues with everyone stripped to their underwear in a plastic kiddy pool. I balanced on the edge of their group, anxiously giddy and enthralled.

It turned out Steve wasn't gay. He dated Andrea for about five years, until she got sick of him. I happened to be back in town that weekend, and in his grief and desperation, he asked me to marry him. "No, I'm serious," he said. When I did get married, he said he was going to come, but he ended up stuck, God knows where, on his bike.

The next time I ran into Steve, I was nine months pregnant with my first child, and he was visiting his mother who was recovering from a hysterectomy—uterine cancer. It was great to see him. He was about to turn forty. His long hair was streaked with grey, he had bulked up a bit, and, to my amazement, he was engaged to be married to a woman with two preteen sons. It seemed that at long last Steve was finally going to grow up. But it never did happen.

Just days before his birthday, months before his wedding, and soon after the birth of my son, Steve was killed in a motorcycle crash. I was shocked and sad, of course, but I also realized that his end eminently fit this eternal child. He had always feared becoming "an aging hipster." Steve's funeral was a reunion of the devotees who had darted in and out of his life—rueful, resentful, adoring, angry, but always, always amused. ◞

Joe and Shirley Gould, New Year's Eve 1939

🐦 From Two to One

by Shirley Gould

CLANG! CLANG! I HEARD THE GEARS as the gravediggers turned the crank to lower Joe's casket into the open grave.

"I can't leave him here!" I cried out to my son Art, the rabbi, whose arm encircled me. Art said, "He's not there, Mom, he's in here, in your heart," and pointed his finger at my chest.

Not until that moment did I fully realize that I was a widow, even though I had already had two days to get used to the idea. Even though I had taken off my wedding ring to remind me: Now I am alone.

A popular Bossa Nova number from the 1960s asked, "Must you dance every dance with the same fortunate man?" I had done that. We fit together well, Joe was a good dancer, and we danced the Double Toddle every chance we got; it fit many different rhythms. Besides, I didn't like to be led by any other man.

Nearly sixty years before, we had pledged to one another and then saved money for two years so we could get married. Together, we'd been through the end of the Great Depression, the start of World War II, and many personal crises. When we finally married in 1940, we knew the draft board would be after him soon. In 1943 the summons arrived, and I was alone for more than two years.

In 1948 our first child, our daughter Ruth, was born, followed enthusiastically by Art nineteen months later. We moved to a brand new house in Skokie, where another son, Shepard, was born to us.

And then, at the age of forty-six, I enrolled in college. Through four years of college and two of grad school, the five of us cooperated to keep our family together and sane. I always knew I wasn't alone in my efforts. On the morning of one of my final exams, Shep, then eight, awoke with a strep throat. Without being asked, Joe got on the phone, changed some business appointments, and volunteered to stay home with Shep until I finished the exam and returned home. That's the kind of partnership our marriage was.

In 1978, when we designed our tallit bag , which I executed in needlepoint and still carry, it never dawned on either of us that one would be left to carry it alone. At the cemetery on that February day in 1999, the reality hit me.

I'd never had a bed of my own as a child, let alone a room of my own. After the crib, I slept in a double bed with an older sister and used the bottom drawer of a shared dresser to hold my few clothes. Now I faced a roomy apartment and the challenge of being part of a community without my guide, my protector, my partner. All those years I assumed that we had friends because Joe was so likeable. Our children preferred him, I thought, and even my family of origin liked him better than they liked me.

However, I knew that life is too precious to spend in sorrow. And I had a lot of learning ahead of me.

The first thing I had to learn was how to fill the gas tank on our car. Handling the checkbook was not quite as difficult. The hardest lesson has been how to be alone, with no one to share ordinary conversation. I hardly watch television, because there is no one on the other side of the room to talk about it with; I don't miss the television, but I do miss the conversation. And it still bothers me that I can look up from the newspaper or book I'm reading and there's no one there to hear my comment.

My family is spread far and wide. Art and his wife live in northern California. Ruth and her husband live in Grand Rapids, Michigan. Shep lives in Lincoln Park, Chicago. I have grandchildren in Israel, Morocco, and Rhode Island, and three in Toronto. As Ruth remarked recently, "You have a serious shortage of hugs."

One of my greatest discoveries has been exercise. We all know how important it is to keep moving. But I grew up a genuine klutz. Gym was the only class I ever failed, and even then I didn't get a D because they didn't want to spoil my honor roll record. Three years ago, however, I was diagnosed with severe spinal stenosis and scoliosis, and the usual treatments didn't alleviate the pain. A personal trainer at the JCC saw my struggles and helped launch me on a program of weight lifting, aerobics, and calisthenics. As a result, my pain is gone, my posture is better, I'm growing more muscles (even after age eighty-four), and my overall health has improved. Also, I have regular opportunities to spend time with congenial people who are also seeking physical activity. My newfound physical fitness offers proof that I can still grow as a person, even alone.

It's no joke to be a widow, but I discovered that life is possible and can even be sweet. Despite the sorrow and loneliness, I have gained a renewed sense of my own worth, an opportunity to give and receive friendship, and a network of younger people who help me when I need it. As all my older siblings die, leaving just one brother, and as my contemporaries continue to pass away, I still have dozens of people who know my name and enjoy my company.

It's a whole new world, and although I didn't choose it, I can and do enjoy it. ❧

Ian Henzel, age 18

⌘ From Shtetl to Shtetl

by Ian Henzel

THE EIFFEL TOWER OF CONEY ISLAND—a parachute jump overlooking the boardwalk and ocean—is one of the iconic images of my childhood in Brighton Beach, Brooklyn. The film that runs in my head is full of these icons: people sitting in front of apartment buildings, sipping tea from glasses and gossiping in Yiddish; small, dark, musty *shuls*, partly illuminated by the orange glow of the memorial plaque lights; streets silent as a tomb on Yom Kippur, when even the Italian pizza places and Chinese restaurants closed for the holiday, only to open at sundown. A place where everyone knew their place and what was expected of them.

"You'll go to a good school, find a nice Jewish girl, get married, and have a good life." My parents repeated this magic formula, as if repetition could will it into reality. My life was planned out when I was just five years old. "Get good grades, so you can go to a good college," my mother told me on my first day of kindergarten. It was all so simple. Follow the rules and there would be *nachas* enough for everyone.

I had my own plans. In family lore about my learning to walk, my excited parents knelt down, arms outstretched to me, calling "E-ala." (This was the Brooklyn Yiddish diminutive for the name Ian, a name that in 1950s Brooklyn was chosen by exactly one family.) I stood up, turned around, and walked away from them. My parents were a bit surprised. "Always running in the opposite direction!" they would come to say. Clearly there was something different about me.

The differences did not go away or get easier to live with. The feeling of not fitting in did not subside. Other boys read the Sunday comics; I read the Sunday apartment rental ads. Other boys played ball; I preferred to read or create things out of construction paper, big dry cell batteries, wires, motors, and lights. Much to my father's disappointment, I never used the baseball glove he bought for my birthday, partly due to my lack of interest, but mainly because of my older brother's passion for throwing softballs at my head.

I do remember other boys and my fascination with them. I wanted to be best friends with Spin and Marty from the *Mickey Mouse Club,* and especially with Will Robinson from *Lost in Space,* with his tousled hair, button nose, and *goyisha punim.* I daydreamed about adventures on distant planets and sleepovers in Will's cabin on the spaceship, Jupiter 2.

I didn't have a name for this at the time. I just liked other boys a lot; I liked being around them, and I wanted them to like me too. I thought that sharing a bed for a sleepover would just be an added feature of our friendship.

Life moved on in the Brighton *shtetl.* My parents sent me to, or, shall I say, had me committed to, a *yeshiva.* I began to understand what my strange feelings were. In the schoolyard, in whispered conversations with friends, and while studying Leviticus in *Chumash* class, I began to acquire a vocabulary to describe them. I got very good at fitting in, and at joining in with the derogatory remarks.

It was clear to my parents that I had no desire to continue at the *yeshiva,* and I was released from bondage into the Brooklyn public high school system, where I managed to fit in, if not with the more popular kids, then at least with a group of somewhat weirder people like myself. I even made several close friends.

But this was New York in the early 1970s. In June 1969, a group of gay men at a gay bar in Greenwich Village fought back during a routine police raid and touched off the Stonewall Riots, five nights of rioting that began the modern gay rights movement. The news even reached the little *shtetl* of Brighton Beach. I read it in the *Village Voice.* On a Saturday late-night public radio program called "Out of the Slough,"

I first heard gay people talk about politics and the process of coming out. There, on Coney Island Avenue, in the dark, I realized that I was not alone.

In June 1973 I graduated from Abraham Lincoln High School and left the *shtetl* for the new world of college. About 9:00 P.M. on Saturday, June 21, 1973, I boarded the "D" train to the city, bound for a dance held by the Gay Activists Alliance in Soho. I had never gone into the city alone that late on a Saturday night. My heart was pounding.

"Maybe I should get off the train at Sheepshead Bay," I thought.

"This is the point of no return," I told myself. "Once you walk in there, you cannot have never been in a gay place. If you meet someone, this all cannot have never happened!" An even more incongruous thought: "What if no one thinks I'm cute?"

I stayed on the train. At the dance, standing in line looking down at my sneakers, I paid my one-dollar admission. I was in an old firehouse with hundreds of other people just like me. I did not have to pretend or hide. For the first time I could remember, I felt comfortable, like I belonged. It was an incredible relief.

I had great hopes that evening that I would meet Will Robinson. Instead, I met a very nice, young, recently ordained rabbi named Barry. My mother, if I could have told her, would have been very happy. Not many boys from the Brighton *shtetl* could go to a gay dance in Soho and wind up with a rabbi. Maybe that was a sign that this was not a monumental change, only a small readjustment, trading an old *shtetl* for a new one.

Like my childhood *shtetl*, there was the warmth and feeling of a real community. But this new *shtetl* replaced dourness with parades and lots of show tunes, men who wore dresses and fussed over me like old *bubbes*, and women who wore tool belts and put up my bookshelves. There was a sense of place and a sense of home—and a sense that, no matter what happens, you can be proud of who you are and rejoice in your life. ❧

Whitefish, Montana

A Mom's Wedding Day Message

by Sallie E. Gratch

IT WAS EARLY SPRING, MARCH 19, 1987; my husband Alan and I were on a Sierra Club Service trip, doing trail maintenance on the North Rim of the Grand Canyon. With fifteen other volunteers available to work the trails, opportunities abounded to slip away from the group and take in the beauty of our surroundings.

I needed the seclusion of a distant canyon for a special reason. In less than one month, my son Joel would be marrying his high school sweetheart, Reese. I felt uneasy as I anticipated one chapter of life ending and another beginning. Had I adequately imparted my values, provided him with ample support and direction? What words did I still want to share?

Filled with these thoughts, I wandered into a nearby canyon and settled myself on the edge of a creek. Towering walls of rock surrounded, calmed, and encouraged me. I pulled paper and pencil from my daypack and soon discovered the words I wanted to share with my son and daughter-in-law on their wedding day.

On Kanab Creek

What can we wish for you?
A life as bright as this day
Perfumed by early spring breezes.
Strength as in these two imposing canyon walls
whose impenetrable sides
make room for the occasional flower or shrub.

See how the river serves to separate ancient rock
And appears as one several bends away.
Life ends here also.
Time-ravaged rocks,
Dry cracked river beds,
Slipped rock faces
Remind us of those who no longer share our joys.
How cold and gloomy this place becomes.
But, in time, the sun teases its way through milk-white clouds
Bringing warmth and renewal to the canyon and the spirit.

We learn from our natural surroundings.
Our lives replicate the beauty around us.

You are like these canyon walls:
Strong, proud, and separate,
Respecting each other's uniqueness
As these rocks have reflected their mutual admiration
throughout the centuries.

All about us is connected.
The rosebud blooms.
A blade of grass interrupts a beetle's lazy stroll.
Your union adds dimension to existing systems,
Welcoming you with love and tenderness.

Change with the seasons.
Make soft places for buds to grow
As these canyon walls enjoy.
Marvel at each other's accomplishments
As if seeing for the first time
the green blush of new leaves
floodlit by the rays of the morning sun.
Stand tall to your principles.
Express your feelings, even when they bring a chill,
But give time to the other to find new footing.
May you find this place many times;
Color-filled, from blue sky to red sand,
Warmed by the sun,
Cooled by the canyon breeze,
Soundless save for the wren's melodic call.
Here is peace.
May it be yours forever. ❧

Sally Heimann Brumer, January 1, 1956

🐦 Jewish Courtship, Small-Town Midwest Style

by Carol Brumer Gliksman

WEDDINGS WERE THE JEWISH matchmaking events of the day in the 1950s, at least in the small Midwestern communities where my parents grew up.

On Memorial Day 1955, in South Bend, Indiana, my father Jerome Brumer and my mother Sally Heimann each came to a wedding that neither had wanted to attend. Sally drove with her parents from Ohio. Jerome discovered that Sally's sister had been his childhood classmate many years earlier at Perley Elementary School in South Bend. Not surprisingly, Jerome's mom, a widow, had known Sally's parents in this tiny, close-knit Jewish community.

When the wedding thrust them back into each other's path, Jerome was a fifth-grade teacher at Franklin Elementary School, and Sally was a college student at Ohio State. Jerome asked Sally's mother if he could escort her home.

One week later, Sally and her mother were traveling to New York on a buying trip for the family store in Ohio. Sally carried a bridal magazine. When her mother asked what it was for, my mother boldly exclaimed that she was going to marry the man she had met at the wedding. Her hunch would prove to be right.

Thus began a several-month courtship, requiring four to five hours of road travel each way prior to four-lane divided highways, between

South Bend, Indiana, and Lima, Ohio. My parents were engaged on Labor Day and married the following New Year's Day.

Their wedding was an elaborate formal affair with six attendants on each side. My grandfather, a furrier, made white rabbit fur muffs for the bridal attendants. And when mom's rabbi became ill, the great Rabbi Maurice Parzen, of blessed memory, drove from South Bend to Lima to conduct the ceremony. Because it was an evening wedding, they broke tradition and had the wedding meal before the ceremony. The photographer from the wedding won a prize with his singular photo of my mother in her wedding gown.

My parents' wedding set off a chain reaction in their circle of friends. Dad's best friend received the name and number of a woman in Cleveland. At their wedding, another couple publicly announced their engagement. And so the networking and matchmaking continued. As I write this, my parents, with God's help, will be married for fifty years this coming New Year's Day, 2006. ✺

◢ My Synagogue Soul Mate

by Beryl Michaels

THE EVENING WAS PLEASANT ENOUGH; a mild breeze made its way across the little meeting room in the old Evanston church. Jews had gathered here to welcome Shabbat this Friday night, a celebration this group had been observing together for several years. I was delightfully surprised by the warm welcome I received, even if it was because my host and hostess were extremely well liked and he was the president of the congregation. During several years of *shul* shopping, I had not received so much as a nod of notice, let alone people actually introducing themselves to me.

The reason for the inattention at other congregations was my singleness. Here I was in my early thirties and I was not one-half of a married couple, past or present.

It was so refreshing to feel included; I was elated. Then the service began. It was totally participatory. The young, newly hired, recently ordained rabbi was thoughtful, personable, and apparently innovative. Never mind his off-key voice: there were others who could carry the tune. Male-gender God references were just beginning to be questioned, so there were lots of on-the-spot language changes.

But then came the best part of the service for me. The rabbi began discussing Reconstructionism—Judaism's youngest branch—and I knew I had found a real spiritual connection.

I had never realized that my secret approach to God had a name, or that my internal translations of some Jewish traditions were shared by others. I uncovered all kinds of commonality between my belief system and the ideas the rabbi presented.

The hot fudge sauce on my sundae came on my next visit to JRC. This time I arrived alone. My hosts from the previous Shabbat were out of town. I was a bit fearful that I would spend the evening in isolation despite the forty people who were there. Boy, was I wrong! I was greeted with the same enthusiasm and warmth as on my first visit. Several couples encouraged me to return. Had I finally found my spiritual home?

Three years after I joined JRC, I was an officer of the board, chairing what was then called the Religious Affairs Committee. Single women and men, lesbian women and gay men, older people and couples of all variations were equally welcomed at this place. Inclusiveness is more common today, as is lip service to that goal, but in the mid-1970s this was a radical philosophy, and I was grateful for it.

Attending Friday night services and Saturday morning *Bnai Mitzvah* became a regular commitment.

When I joined the ranks of Jewish communal professionals in 1981, I found myself visiting other Jewish communities across the country. Frequently, my work took me to synagogues for Shabbat services, where I recognized that my familiarity with liturgy, regardless of the synagogue's affiliation, came directly from my active membership at JRC.

Then I began attending the Saturday morning *minyan*. For the first time ever, I chanted Torah and was called as a Bat Mitzvah. I went to Israel for the International Jewish Feminist Conference in 1988, and there I became one of the first "women of the wall." Seventy or so women joined in an extraordinary weekday morning prayer service at the Western Wall. It was the first time in Israel's history that women had held their own Torah service at this holy site. Because I had so often wrapped and unwrapped our JRC Torah scrolls on Saturday morning at *minyan*, I knew what to do during this service. I stood next to each of the three women who received an *aliyah* as they chanted Torah for the first time ever at this holiest of holy places. It was my personal privilege to hold steady first one, then

John Bach and Beryl Michaels, March 28, 1993

the next, and finally the third as each woman found herself shaking to be davening in that space.

The sense of belonging that I felt at JRC laid the foundation for my career as a Jewish communal professional and provided a backdrop for my venture into other realms of Jewish life. JRC was my refuge when I was painfully needy. It was where I celebrated my marriage after I finally met my husband. It is where I return whenever I need a spiritual lift. It is truly my synagogue soul mate. ⤴

≈ Mother Marries Son!

by Charlene Gelber

DID YOU SEE THAT HEADLINE IN THE *National Enquirer?*
As a Jewish groom and a bride with no religious preference, my son
and future daughter-in-law decided on a Jewish officiant for their
wedding.

While interviewing potential marriage officiants, they discovered
that their home state of California sanctions marriages performed
by lay persons if they have filled out the required form and presented
themselves to be deputized in court.

"Hullo, Ma. Monica and I want you to perform our marriage. Would
you marry us?"

"What! What! Are you kidding? You want me to do what?"

After the initial shock, I felt like Sally Fields accepting the Academy
Award: "You like me, you really like me."

I conferred with my husband and other two children.

My analytical middle child asked, "Well, how do you feel about it?"

"I'm not a rabbi, lawyer, or judge: where do I come off doing this?"

"Oh, but Mom, to us you are all those things."

I accepted my son and his fiancee's flattering offer and began
researching wedding ceremonies. I was excited. It felt so JRC to be
planning a member-led service. We chose prayers and readings that
fit into the basic structure of a Jewish wedding. I created and wrote a
ceremony especially for the bridal couple.

My swearing-in appointment was set for the Thursday before the wedding. I entered a conference room in the Los Angeles County Recorder of Deeds building. Seven others were also waiting for instructions on becoming official marriage officiants. The actual title to be bestowed upon us was Deputy Commissioner of Civil Marriages. I wanted to add "Lord High" to the title and break into an operetta.

We were told what we had to say during the ceremony, and how to fill out the marriage certificate to solemnize the marriage and make it legal. Then we all stood up, raised our right hands, and took the oath. We swore to uphold the Constitution of the United States and the Constitution of the State of California, to defend our borders from foes, not to commit treason, and serious stuff like that. I prayed no foes would show up, but to be safe, I planned to station a civil defense team at the shoreline just down the hill from the wedding. If enemies appeared, I would use my limited Hebrew and shout, "epho, epho" (there, there).

Back to the courthouse. My formerly talkative group of fellow deputies grew somber and quiet. Taking that oath affected us. The older gentleman sitting next to me said that the last time he raised his hand and took an oath, he was gone for five years. We wished each other well and departed. With the vision of a big metal deputy star pinned to my chest, and a set of six shooters complementing my pearl necklace and diamond earrings, I was ready to do the deed in my new capacity as a Deputy Commissioner of Civil Marriages.

The wedding day came. When the florist arrived, he was wearing a *kippah*.

"The florist at my son's wedding is wearing a *kippah*, but my son isn't," I told him.

He gave me a weird look. I explained the situation, knowing he thought I was somewhat nuts.

"Who's doing the wedding?" he asked.

"I am," I replied.

"Are you having a rabbi?" he responded.

Again I said, "I'm doing the wedding."

Boy, was his *kippah* spinning.

Monica & Jason's wedding, July 4, 2000

The reality of what I was about to do fell over me like a prayer shawl. I was legally joining my son and the woman he loved in a civil marriage. But it felt so Jewish: the learning process, the questions raised, the interpretations discussed. Not to mention the emotional process: the spirit engaged and the love released. We even had a booklet.

The ceremony was great: an all-American politically correct marriage of a secular Jewish groom and a non-religious Mexican-American bride, on the Fourth of July. This was not an interfaith wedding, my son enlightened me, for the two of them share the same deep belief in God. They just got there from different places. An idea from a children's book helped them express this melding of their backgrounds. Attached to the guests' table cards were jalapeño bagels.

It was a delightful wedding, filled with warmth, love, and a wonderful feeling of creating the perfect event for this beautiful and unique couple. I was proud of their creativity, their passion for each other, and their courage to do something different. Their love and faith in me were overwhelming. My gift to them was to write and perform their wedding ceremony, a mother's unusual send-off into matrimony. Their gift to me—their respect and trust—was even greater. It was a very proud moment for our family, a family whose life has been blessed with love. ᴥ

✿ Ten Things I've Learned from My Orthodox Son

by Jeff Winter

NEITHER MY WIFE NOR I WOULD HAVE expected that, from the lively blend of traditional and liberal Judaism they experienced at home, one of our children would embrace a strict form of traditional observance. Joshua's journey to Orthodox Judaism began about six years ago, while he was in high school. His transition became ours as well.

Now that Josh is raising his own family, deeply committed to Orthodoxy, my wife Sally and I find ourselves in a curious position as parents and grandparents. It's not what we expected, but at least now we understand that old saying, "People plan and God laughs."

Here are just ten of the many things I've learned from my son's journey to Orthodox Judaism:

1. The chosen people are choosy.
   Serious soul searching precedes the decision to adopt a modern Orthodox, Zionist, *Lubavitch,* or *Haredi* lifestyle. One must grapple with whether to extend the wardrobe beyond black and white, whether or not to own or use a television, how to cover one's hair (*sheitel* or snood), and which rabbinic certification or *kashrut* to hold by. The spectrum of choices is wide, and the decisions affect the family's communal, academic, social, and spiritual life.

2. The *dybbuk* is in the details.

   Even a master's degree in Jewish studies and more than twenty years teaching Jewish subjects offered me little help in understanding the endless principles and arcane minutiae of Shabbat observance. When my son's family spends Shabbat with us, I try to make the environment appropriately *Shabbasdik*. Still, questions abound: do I add instant coffee to the hot water or the other way around? What do I do before Shabbat to that porch light that goes on with a motion sensor? Fortunately, I always remember to unscrew the bulb in the fridge late Friday afternoon so we can eat.

3. *Davening* can fill up a day.

   For many Orthodox Jews, praying thrice daily builds a community of spirit and fellowship and deepens a personal relationship with God. *Davening* structures time and makes the rhythms of Jewish life pervasive. But it also interferes with many other plans; and, for those of us who aren't daily *daveners*, it can be a bit tedious. Personally, many mornings, rather than wrap *tefillin*, I work out or jog. I don't know if this is why, but my son seems to be the one gaining weight.

4. Regular *daveners* get there faster.

   I'm fortunate to have the skills necessary to participate in traditional *Shacharit, Mincha,* and *Ma'ariv* services, but I'm often awed by the lightening speed of prayers. At times I've missed entire sections while searching for the right page. As far as knowing the entire canon of prayer ritual, it takes a lifetime to learn the rules, and, I think, another fifty years to learn the exceptions.

5. Everybody still loves Saturday night.

   Now that our son is Orthodox, though, it's taken on a new meaning in our home. Attending Shabbat *Mincha* and *seudah shlishit* (the third meal) really cuts into Saturday night plans, particularly in July when Shabbat ends close to 10 P.M. That's why it's a good idea to nap in the afternoon after enjoying the *cholent*. Those slow hours are a wonderful time for walking and talking.

6. Don't touch those hot buttons.

   I can still discuss many things with Josh and his friends, but I've learned to avoid God, Torah, and Israel (the people and the land). Suffice it to say that political discourse between red states and blue states is softball compared to debates about the Big Three.

7. You never know who's coming to dinner.

   Last summer after hosting a cookout for Josh and his friends, I was shocked to discover that I had just fed a small group of Republicans. But it was only one meal and some of it was overcooked. And, of course, I was also feeding my son.

8. It takes a *shtetl.*

   Orthodox groups offer each other a deep and pervasive support, with *gemach,* or free loan societies, providing everything from strollers and playpens to wedding meals and apartments. The depth of care within this community should make outsiders envious.

9. Bite your tongue.

   My son's journey continually re-sensitizes me to the power of spoken words and deeds. I have never heard my son or his friends use profanity, engage in gossip, or glorify sexist, shallow media-driven entertainment or sexist images. These positive outcomes stem from avoiding much within popular culture, and I benefit from the reminder.

10. Meet your new teachers.

    I may not choose to view the world through Orthodox lenses, but I can still appreciate the growth my son and his family have experienced from embracing traditional Judaism. My son has become my teacher and guide as I watch and occasionally join their trip. Supporting this journey that connects me to Josh, Liz, and their impressive children is a foundation of deep, abiding love. It lends a dynamic and spiritual backdrop to this puzzling, challenging, and enriching drama we call life. ❧

❧ The One-Day Seder Miracle

by Marie Davidson

RECENT CONVERTS TEND TO THROW themselves into their new life path energetically and with a certain naivete, and I was no exception. It was barely a year after I went to the *mikvah,* and I was approaching my first Passover as an official Jew. Having been to a number of Seder*s* at my mother-in-law's home, I decided, in a giddy flush of enthusiasm, to invite my in-laws to our home for the Seder. I had pulled off any number of Easter dinners, Christmas feasts, and experimental ethnic extravaganzas. How hard could this be?

I had no idea.

I carefully boxed up all our *chametz* and lugged it to the basement storage locker of our "cozy" graduate student apartment in Hyde Park. The apartment was cramped, with no true dining area, and its railroad-car-type kitchen had almost no counter space. I knew our home would present logistical problems for the Seder, but I was a cock-eyed optimist. In my heart, I knew that what mattered most was the spirit of the event and how welcome our guests would feel.

My husband Larry thought it was a fine idea to invite his family, but he was his father's son ("can't find a glass in the kitchen or the water," according to my mother-in-law), so I was on my own. We had eight guests plus us, to make ten. Parents-in-law, two sisters-in-law, an aunt, a cousin and his wife, and, most important, the grandmother.

Grandmother "Non," a petite and birdlike woman, was a master cook and a shrewd businesswoman. She had left the pogroms of Eastern Europe as a young girl and never looked back. Once, while recovering from surgery at Northwestern Hospital, she shooed her doctor away while she was on the phone, scolding "Can't you see I'm doing business here?" Despite her heart condition, Non still did the turkey and stuffing for holiday meals and brought it in a newspaper-insulated laundry basket.

Fool that I was, I didn't think to ask Non to bring turkey to my Seder. No, I was going to do it all, from fish to macaroons. I had my guide, *The Jewish Festival Cookbook (According to the Dietary Laws)* by Fannie Engle and Gertrude Blair. Equally important, I had what I now call "clueless Gentile chutzpah."

First, I planned the menu. I figured on turkey, because I had roasted turkeys and knew enough to take out the bag containing the organs and gizzard. And I remembered how much work it was to do a turkey. From my Jewish cookbook, I picked out a recipe for carrot *tzimmes*. My in-laws, who were all probably wondering how *meshuggie* their new relative was, had kindly insisted on bringing things—a potato *kugel*, a salad, a dessert. My next big decision was whether to make chicken soup from scratch. I decided I had to, but I could compromise and make matzo balls from the Manischewitz mix. I did have enough sense to know that making homemade gefilte fish would be insane. Instead, I got Non's suggestion for the best commercial brand (Mother's) and type (sweet).

I did my shopping. Larry and I borrowed folding tables and chairs from the neighbors in our apartment building. I hauled out some tablecloths and serving pieces. I looked again at my one-person kitchen with no counters and no dishwasher, and opted for paper plates—sturdy pretty ones. We would have real flatware, although I had to borrow some to have enough. Larry was in charge of the Haggadah; the intellectual part of the holiday was his turf.

As a graduate student busy with courses and papers, I let the real preparation go until the morning of the Seder. As I now know, it is impossible to make a Seder in one day. As the morning progressed, I gradually realized that I had neither the time nor the space to get it all done. I was overextended up to my eyeballs. Larry saw that I was somewhere beyond frantic and pitched in to set up the tables. I took a deep breath and reminded myself that guests will forgive a lot if the spirit is right. Then I jettisoned the soup and the matzo balls. Fish would have to be enough. The turkey, stuffed with a savory crushed matzo stuffing, smelled divine. I prepared the *tzimmes* so it was oven-ready.

Then I turned my attention to the Seder plate. A roasted lamb bone? *Oy*. (I was beginning to use *oy* a lot that day. It felt very natural.) A roasted turkey bone would work just as well. The huge club-like piece of horseradish was an absolute bear to peel and cut—a rutabaga with attitude. Oh, no, hard-boiled eggs! Larry was sent on an emergency mission to buy more eggs. Parsley to dip, salt water, carve the turkey. Twenty minutes to showtime, I realized I had forgotten the *charoset*. *Oy gevalt*. Larry went out on a mercy mission to beg walnuts. *Charoset* without a food processor certainly involves a lot of chopping. I was very grateful that our guests were late.

Somehow, the Red Sea parted, and I squeaked through. As we sat down, our guests looked with shock at the paper plates, a clear deviation from holiday protocol. But converts can get away with a lot, I have learned. Twenty-five years and many Seders later, I still use paper and still get away with it. A few guests did miss the soup but were understanding, even incredulous, when I told them about my one-day effort. My mother-in-law raved about the *tzimmes*, and she still tells me every year that I have never been able to duplicate it. Whether beginner's luck or clueless Gentile chutzpah, everyone enjoyed the Seder, the food was good, and the discussion was lively. I was pleased. Our small apartment was filled with holiday *ruach*.

But the best part was when Non gave me a big hug as she left, and said, in her Yiddish-accented English, "Well, you are a real *balaboste!*" ❧

✒ There's No Going Home Again

by Cheryl Bondy Kaplan

WHEN MY PARENTS ANNOUNCED THAT they were planning to move out of the house in which I grew up, I was thrilled for them. Built in the 1930s but stuck in a 1970s décor freeze frame, the home showed its age. My parents seemed paralyzed about making any substantive changes or improvements, preferring to peek behind bedroom doors and see the lurking ghosts of teenage pasts. My two sisters and I were all grown and out of the house, and this would give my parents a fresh start. They were still young, and while many of their friends were downsizing to condos and smaller homes, Mom and Dad decided to look for a larger home in which they could more comfortably entertain their growing brood.

My parents conducted a frustrating multi-year search that shattered their real estate broker's previous record for the most indecisive clients. Convinced that walking up and down stairs would be their undoing as they grew older, they were determined to find a ranch house, real estate jargon for a one-story residence. Apparently ranch houses in the northern Chicago suburbs were few and far between. Finally, after years of looking at hundreds of houses, they found The One. The new home's basement featured a genuine replica of Trader Vic's Polynesian Tiki Room, which is simultaneously magnificent and kitsch, and which my parents embraced with gusto. Since they host most of their large family gatherings in this basement

Karen, Lila, and Cheryl Bondy, 1966

room, ironically, the stairs that they were running away from are still very much in their lives. So far, this has not caused their ruin.

My parents sold their house in a handshake deal to the lovely young family that lived next door. In preparation for the move, Mom gave us a firm deadline after which all unclaimed belongings my sisters and I had left, dumped, or deserted at their old house would be thrown or given away. Over the next months we hauled high school yearbooks, old 45s, photo albums, and wedding dresses from the old homestead's basement and closets to our respective apartments and houses.

I had expected to feel depressed saying goodbye to the home I had moved into when I was only four. I had thought it would be painful to give up the yellow room with the gingham curtains in which I spent my formative years. But instead, I felt cleansed and mature. I was relieved that this transition was taking place while my parents were in good health; moving all of those belongings under different circumstances would have been much more difficult.

But something unexpected happened to me when Mom and Dad moved into their new home. I didn't realize this until they were settled in, and it still hits me every time I walk through their front door. I now feel completely different visiting them. I no longer go home, I go to visit my parents. And that is a huge distinction. There was something nurturing and comforting about stepping into the old house. The old house had a smell and an aura that embraced me and swept me back to a simpler time, to childhood.

Entering the old house, I could make a beeline for the junk drawer and find the cinnamon gum that I would chew only during those visits. I could navigate the place blindfolded. I could plop down on my old bed and recall with nostalgia late-night sleepovers with my friends. Even though they have lived in their "new" house for over fifteen years, try as I might, I still can't seem to remember where the can opener is. So I'm not much help in the kitchen. And I've given up looking for the cinnamon gum.

Still, I would not choose to alter the course of events. My parents have flourished in their new surroundings. Mom loves her large yard and garden; Dad now has his own office, a significant upgrade from the card table that served as an ad hoc desk in their old bedroom. Nevertheless, I regret that some things can't be boxed up and loaded onto a moving van, and I'll probably always miss the little piece of me that remained behind on Birchwood Avenue. ❧

Bobbie Berkowitz, November 2003

How Israel Converted Me

by Bobbie Berkowitz

UNTIL 1991, MY VACATION OF CHOICE was not Israel, but London. It had family, great theater, and an understandable language, none of which I'd find in Israel.

Of course, I recall the excitement when Israel declared itself an independent state. And I remember following the news during the Six-Day War in 1967; watching TV coverage of the 1972 Olympic massacre; and sitting in synagogue on Yom Kippur 1973, waiting to hear the latest on the surprise attack on Israel. But for many years Israel had little personal meaning for me, a non-religious Jew in America. It was Palestine where my grandfather had worked before coming to Chicago, and Palestine on the beautiful certificate showing where family friends planted trees in my honor when I was born. Israel seemed very far away and long ago. Though I supported the country and was proud of its accomplishments, I had no interest in traveling there.

My husband Barry had always wanted to visit Israel. In 1991, the year of the first Iraq war with its Scud missiles, he finally talked me into going there for two weeks. By a stroke of luck we had a private guide who took us to places tourists rarely see.

Ten years later we returned with a small group sponsored by Northwestern University's Chabad. In addition to becoming reacquainted with "first-timer" sites, we climbed in nature parks, toured David Ben Gurion's home, rode donkeys in an ancient Galilee setting, and swayed on slow-moving camels in a Druze camp. A euphoric feeling lingered, and we excitedly told our stories to anyone who would listen.

From the day we arrived home, we were determined to go back in two years. The next time we went to Israel, we were in the Army. *Sar-El*, Volunteers for Israel, is a program for people who want to spend at least two weeks working at a military base. Four-star hotels were just for the weekend. Five days a week we wore Army uniforms, handled our assigned jobs, ate meals with soldiers in the mess halls, and slept in separate barracks. We also became friends with group members from different countries and of different religions. We look forward to reliving this experience when we re-enlist.

Since our first visit in 1991, my interest in Israel has deepened beyond that of a tourist or volunteer. E-mails, Internet links, and newspapers keep me in touch and help balance the many troubles of the state with its inspiring successes in science and technology. Studying the Bible and learning Jewish history have also become more meaningful now that I've seen some of the sites.

Vacation means Israel to me now that I've been converted from a casual well-wisher to one of that country's many unofficial ambassadors. ⮜

Third Time's the Charm

by Carol Ellegant

WHEN I WAS GROWING UP IN Huntington, West Virginia, I felt sorry for the Jewish boys. For their Bar Mitzvahs, they had to learn Hebrew, chant from the Torah, and then stand in front of the entire congregation and give a speech. I was much too shy to imagine standing on the *bima* saying anything at all, let alone chanting Torah and giving a speech.

As for a Bat Mitzvah, such a thing simply wasn't being done then where I came from. In fact, growing up in the 1940s and 1950s, I'd never even heard of a Bat Mitzvah.

But even though I wasn't destined to have a Bat Mitzvah, my parents insisted on sending me to study Hebrew with our rabbi. So twice a week for a year or two, I rode my bike after school to the synagogue a good distance away. The boys, who studied with the sad-looking little *chazzan*, seemed to be reading the entire Bible and having interesting discussions. Meantime, as the only girl attending Hebrew School, I plodded along with the rabbi, an indifferent teacher. I had trouble learning the Hebrew letters and never connected them into words to read with any fluency.

Years later, as an adult and a new member of JRC, I got a second chance to learn Hebrew, not because my parents insisted, but because I wanted to. The teacher, one of JRC's founders, boasted a good track record of teaching congregants to read. In this class, though, we took

Carol Ellegant, November 2004

turns trying and failing to read various passages. I felt stressed and embarrassed but tried to hide my disappointment by telling myself, "I've never been good with languages, so why should this time be any different?"

But then, fifteen years later, another Hebrew class was offered, billed for "people who can't learn Hebrew." I certainly fit into that category, so I registered and began to attend. At the beginning and end of each class, we chanted, "I can learn Hebrew." Our teacher Bruce wrote Beatles song titles and other phrases phonetically on the board in Hebrew so we could get used to the strange letters. To give us confidence, we never had to read alone, but always read as a class. The book and accompanying tapes for adult learners were user-friendly. We made flash cards. I even began to study outside of class. Bruce said fifteen minutes daily, and that's what I did every morning before I left for work. I was finally learning to read Hebrew.

When a new adult B'nai Mitzvah class was announced, I began to study with a supportive, committed group of other adults who had never had a Bar or Bat Mitzvah in their youth. We met faithfully every Monday night for a year and a half. We studied not only Hebrew, but also the year's cycle of Jewish holidays, the prayer book, the Shabbat service, and other Jewish topics that came up in class.

My Bat Mitzvah allowed me to lead songs and prayers, chant from the Torah, write an essay for a booklet about my Torah portion, and even make a speech about why I wanted a Bat Mitzvah at that point in my life. With family and friends in attendance, this was one of the most fulfilling events of my life. The Jewish boys of Huntington, West Virginia, would have envied me. ❧

❧ Late Start

by Maxine Topper

WAY TO GO, MA! FOUR WORDS, written by my son on my brand new spiral notebook. The notebook, a gift from a friend, was accompanied by two new pencils, sharpened just right. Armed with these items, I nervously entered the classroom to begin the classes to complete my bachelor's degree. The dress I wore was a little out of place next to the jeans and torn tee shirts my fellow students were wearing. I was forty.

At forty-three I took another walk—this time down the aisle to receive my diploma, amidst cheers from my family and friends. Moving that beautiful tassel from one side to the other brought feelings of pride, relief, and pleasure that will forever be part of my memories. I felt a sense of accomplishment as grand as what Rocky must have felt running up the stairs of the Pennsylvania Art Museum—raising his arms in the air and exclaiming, "Yo, Adrian, I did it!" The movement of the tassel represented the next step, a door opening to the rest of my professional life. That day was the fulfillment of a dream that I had carried since I left Michigan State University, quietly, a month before the end of my sophomore year. I was eighteen.

Many times I had dreamed about returning to school, trying again, smiling as the Provost handed me my diploma with a handshake and congratulations. But each time, I awoke with the renewed fear and memory of my early disappointments. Though the prospect of taking classes and maneuvering a university system on top of my family and job seemed a bit overwhelming, I carried that dream until the time was right, until I felt ready—and I ran out of reasons not to.

I realized I needed to complete my education when I was turned down for a job because I lacked a bachelor's degree. I was told all I needed was a program that would allow me to "get my ticket punched." I didn't really need a major; my work experience would speak for itself. So began my journey, at midlife, to finish what I had started many years before. This time, though, I had a little more self-confidence and self-discipline and a lot more maturity. As I began to research possibilities, college catalogs began to pile up, and I evaluated programs, costs, and options for financial aid. This time I was determined not to fail. This time I would graduate.

I started at Oakton College, where I completed a few courses to earn my A.A. degree.

After Oakton, I enrolled in an alternative degree program at National Louis University that allowed me to earn credit for life experience. I wrote essay after essay, matching past experiences with course requirements. I studied for and passed exams that gave credits for basic courses that I was missing, and I took classes in a variety of disciplines to reach the 120 credits I needed to finish.

Referred to as an "adult learner," I learned a lot. I learned that older students were generally more interested in the content of the course than were younger students, who focused on the minimum requirements to obtain the best grade. I learned that an older mind, cluttered with thoughts of aging parents and children's car pools, has a harder time retaining information. I learned about myself and I learned about the world. I learned how to study, and I learned how smart I really was.

Returning to school in mid-life, with a husband, children, a job, and the responsibility of aging parents, was a challenge. Finding time and a quiet place to study, write papers, and do research was difficult. I carried books everywhere. Since I was easily distracted at home, I would sometimes study at my mom's, nourished by her need to bring me tea, falling into patterns from high school. As an overachieving, trying-to-prove-something student, I often let five-page assignments become fifteen-page papers. Some long papers were composed in the parking lots of forest preserves. I would sit in the back seat of my car, the only quiet place in my life at that time.

Maxine Topper,
June 10, 1980

My daughter, son, and husband were wonderfully supportive, encouraging me and taking over household responsibilities as my time for those chores became limited. Somehow they kept clean and fed, and laundry got done. They studied with me, read and edited papers, shlepped books, and told their friends about me. My self-confidence grew as each class was completed, and my grades reflected my efforts. I began to believe that a whole new world of professional opportunity might now be a possibility.

When all the papers had been turned in, the research completed, and the books closed, I knew that for that moment, as I joined my classmates in the auditorium, I was enjoying my fifteen minutes of fame. We smoothed our gowns in anticipation of marching in to "Pomp and Circumstance." As the music played and we entered the auditorium, I greedily searched the audience for the faces of my family and friends. They were there, bathing me with smiles and high fives. I smiled back, filled with pride for myself and others in my class who had overcome large challenges to arrive at this day. I remembered that the motto of my high school graduating class had been "The door to success is labeled *push.*" Twenty-five years later, I proudly walked through that door. ❧

With All My Heart and All My Soul

by Rhonda Present

THE *VE'AHAVTA* PRAYER CHARGES US to love God with all our heart and all our soul. The way a child loves a mother. The way a mother loves her child.

In 2004 I celebrated my fortieth birthday and the tenth anniversary of my reunion with the extraordinary woman who gave me life. This story is for her.

My birth mother Ellen was just twenty-one when I was born in 1964. She was college educated and self-supporting. But she was also a single parent, which was not condoned by her traditional Jewish family. My father had died during her pregnancy, and it did not help that he was of Moroccan descent and a non-Jew. After nearly a year of fighting to keep me, amidst tremendous pressure from family and Jewish social service professionals, Ellen finally relinquished her parental rights.

I was adopted by a New York Jewish couple who were unable to conceive a child of their own. I always knew that I was adopted and was continually reminded of how special I was to have been "chosen." But despite these positive messages, a question lurked deep inside me: "If I were so special, why would my mother have given me up?" When I asked about my birth family, my parents said they knew little except that my mother was Jewish and had red hair.

During adolescence, my search for identity intensified. Like the little bird that fell from the nest in one of my favorite childhood books, I'd look in crowds for red-headed women who resembled me and wonder, "Are you my mother?"

Little did I know that Ellen was wondering, too. Just a few years after I was placed for adoption, she had married a childhood friend and psychiatrist who encouraged her to contact my adoptive parents. She tried repeatedly throughout the years to get information from the adoption agency. After many failed attempts, she gave up, convinced that perhaps it was best not to interfere in my life.

Even after having two more daughters and building a new family of her own, Ellen never forgot about me. Each year on my birthday, overwhelmed with sadness, she would mourn her loss behind closed doors. Yet she continued to hope that perhaps some day I would look for her, and she never moved far from the Upper West Side neighborhood where she had lived when I was born.

By the time I left home for college, I knew that I needed to search for her. But it would be years before I mustered the courage. I attended a few meetings of an adoptee support group on campus and continued to ask my parents for information. Finally, they gave me a letter that they had received from the adoption agency in 1983. It purported to describe my story, but, as I would later learn, some of the details were inaccurate, and many were missing.

As the Louise Wise agency was robbing me of my rightful history, it was creating one of its own for falsifying the records of many other adoptees. In the late 1990s, this agency, which finally closed its doors last year, was brought to justice when the parents of Michael Juman sued them for withholding information about the mental illness of his birth mother and father. The truth might have saved Michael's life. It would also have prevented the years of pain that my family had to endure.

In my late twenties, after experiencing complications from a minor surgery that resulted in my being diagnosed with a hereditary bleeding disorder, I finally decided to move forward. I had also recently married and was beginning to think about starting a family of my own, further fueling my desire to find my roots.

So, with little information but lots of support from my husband and a wonderful network of birth parents and adoptees, I embarked on my search. An Orthodox Jewish woman in New York became my guide in navigating the underground railroad that would open the door to my past. After a year-long process of combing through birth and death records and making cold calls to cemeteries and possible relations, I finally had the name of the woman I believed was my birth mother. I wrote her a letter, which was hand-delivered by my New York friend.

I will never forget the day in spring 1994 when Ellen called me at work to confirm that she was, indeed, the one I had been looking for. Several months later, she flew to Chicago for our reunion. I also vividly recall that moment at O'Hare Airport when I saw her coming down the escalator and we finally embraced.

It's hard to believe that more than a decade has passed since that day. In many ways, we are still getting to know each other, but sometimes when we pick up the phone to chat about everyday things—the stresses of motherhood or juggling work and family life—it feels as if we were never apart.

Of course, we cannot get back the time stolen from us—years of kissed scraped knees and Bat Mitzvah and wedding celebrations. But we have nevertheless been blessed with a special friendship, unencumbered by the emotions that so often complicate mother-daughter relationships.

Perhaps my most cherished gift has been reclaiming branches of our family tree for my daughter Jorie, who is blessed to have Great-Grandma Selma, Nana Ellen, Papa Ted, and Aunts Kiki and Katrina in her life. In 2002, we were all together for the first time at Kiki's high school graduation. I had only to see the joy on Jorie's face and hear her laughter as she skipped down the streets of Manhattan holding hands with her adoring aunts to feel the fulfillment of a fervent prayer. My prayer.

I prayed to find my birth mother. And I love her with all my heart and all my soul. ❧

◐ My Life Began at Forty

by Joan Spigelman

WHEN I WAS IN SCHOOL, THEY DIDN'T diagnose what I had as a learning disability. Instead, they called me dumb and sat me in the sixth row, last seat. Even my parents told me that I was pretty and sweet, but not very bright.

Beneath my beautiful appearance, I carried a deep sense of shame and a secret. My father was sometimes violent. He had sexually abused me. I barely finished high school, and I married at eighteen, just one week out of school.

By age forty, I had four children and a failing marriage. I had no career, no money, and no means of financial or emotional support. When someone remarked, "Oh, look, beautiful Joannie has wrinkles around her eyes," I wondered how I would survive. For most of my life, I had thought that the only thing I had going for me was my looks.

But I was wrong. In fact, my life would begin at forty.

Five years earlier, my youngest child had been diagnosed as learning disabled. My struggle to win appropriate schooling for him pitted me against my husband, who was ashamed of his son's disability and blamed it on me; against a pediatrician who considered me a crazy mother; and against a school that wanted to hold him back for an extra year in kindergarten.

That struggle revealed my tenacity. I learned that I could appeal to people and they would to listen to me. And, for the first time, I began

Joan and Zaida (front, fourth and fifth from left), c. 1942

to appreciate my native intelligence. When I volunteered in my son's school, I came up with creative ways to help children with learning disabilities. This volunteer work helped me recognize the source of my own learning problems.

So I signed up for my first college course, "The Psychology of Personal Growth." I was terrified. I could hear my mother's voice warning, "Don't try; you can't do it." But in this class I learned that even though the other women could write and spell—things that still give me trouble—I had my own kind of intuitive understanding.

One of the most valuable things I learned in that first class was about mentors. My first mentor had been Zaida, my grandfather. When I was a little girl, I would come home from school and put my head on the radiator, where he would tap a tune for me. Zaida spoke no English, but I knew that he loved me deeply.

Succeeding in this first college class gave me the confidence to try another. When the new class began, I told the teacher I couldn't do the writing he required because of my learning disability. He replied, "I want you to use this journal. You can draw pictures or doodle instead of writing." He also asked if I'd ever used a tape recorder to explain myself, and he told me, "I'll work with you if you work with me." He became another mentor for me, the first of a long line as I continued my studies.

This is why I say my life began at forty. By then, I had begun my studies in earnest. I eventually earned my master's degree in social work from the University of Chicago, the first learning-disabled student ever accepted into their program.

Just ten years after taking my first psychology course, I returned to Oakton Community College to teach that very course. And even now, years later, in my work with individuals and groups, I still try to do as my mentors did. Beginning with Zaida, they all saw beyond my disabilities and my beauty to things I couldn't yet see in myself. A good mentor can help you turn a lifetime of bad into something good. Even when you don't begin until forty. ❧

 Donna

by Darlene Grossman

JULY 24, 1989, 6:00 P.M.

"Can't talk," Mom says.

"Kids there?"

"Right."

"What are the results?" No answer.

"Is it . . . ?"

"Right. . . ."

Since adolescence, I have struggled to separate from my identical twin, Donna, who introduces me jokingly as her Spare Kidney. The irony is that now, at age forty-two, we're being forcibly separated, and there are no parts I can give her.

With the confirmation of her illness, my world changes from technicolor to black and white. The ground I'm standing on begins to shake and tremble, and I do, too. It's the start of a long, uphill journey, which begins in pain, anger, and denial.

JULY 25, 1989

Donna looks as pale as the hospital sheets. They removed a lobe of her lung and plan to check her lymph nodes for further signs of cancer. "If you're going to cry, just leave right now," she begins. Then her voice breaks. "This is it," she says. "This is the end."

"You don't know that," I respond, feeling an ache in my chest.

"I do. When I asked the doctor if I'll live to see my son's Bar Mitzvah in May, he said there were no guarantees."

"I love you," I say out loud for the first time.

"I love you, too," she answers.

AUGUST 1989

My family of origin is stoic. Bottle up the sorrow, the rage, the fear, the love. Cloak them in sarcasm or silence. Whatever the cost, do not let them out. But now my feelings are spilling over. Fine one minute, I rant the next. "Keep busy; don't think!" becomes my new mantra.

MID-SEPTEMBER 1989

I am welcomed into the grief counselor's office. "This time and space," she explains, "are yours. It's safe. Whatever you say is between us. I have big shoulders and can help ease your load."

I breathe a sigh of relief.

She listens patiently, then responds, "Your family is acting out 'The Emperor's New Clothes.' You're pointing out that he's naked, and they're denying that anything is wrong."

My first homework assignment: regular diet, regular sleep, regular exercise. And most challenging: fifteen minutes a day of pleasure.

MARCH 1990

Donna asks me to calligraph the invitations for the Bar Mitzvah. I look over the ones she's done. The shakiness of the letter forms, the steady deterioration between the successive envelopes provide tangible evidence that the cancer is spreading.

"Perhaps the doctors' predictions are wrong," I offer.

"No," Donna replies. She mentions August. As an afterthought she adds, "I'd like to die on Shabbat."

"Do you believe in life after death?" I persist.

"If I didn't, this would be much harder."

"Do me a favor," I joke. "Keep your hands off my lights."

The cancer keeps growing. Weekly, I relay information about Donna's treatments and medications to my therapist. She translates into terms I can understand.

"Adenocarcinoma. They name the cell type but still can't find the primary site."

"Tell me what will happen at the end," I ask, naively believing that I can prepare myself and lessen the pain.

She begins slowly. "Metastasize . . . glands, bones, brain. Eat less . . . sleep more. Lapses into and out of unconsciousness . . . system shut down . . . involuntary reflexes."

I sit with eyes shut tightly, arms pulled over my head, fighting to keep things in. "Dying is a natural process," she says gently. I begin sobbing and she holds me.

Donna and I talk about death, the idea of creating a lasting memory. I offer to videotape her. No, she'll leave her children letters. "And I'm working on my eulogy, too," she adds. "Everyone will be laughing."

MAY 1990, BAR MITZVAH DAY

Donna has willed herself to this day. Because she can no longer sit comfortably, we arrive late at the service. I help her down the aisle, feeling all eyes on us. Her middle son is called to the Torah, and she watches with tears of sadness and joy.

At the luncheon following, she stands for the last time. Donna toasts her son and thanks each person who has helped her. This is her swan song.

The next morning she moves to our parents' home and into my old room to die. From this point on, she is bedridden.

"Why does everyone say she looks great? I think she looks sick, like she's dying!"

"What they mean," my shrink explains patiently, "is that she doesn't look as bad as they imagined she would."

She's aging before my eyes; I see her, my living reflection, growing old. I look often into mirrors now, perhaps to convince myself I'm still here.

JUNE 1, 1990

Our forty-third birthday. I bring Donna the only gift she can use—a nightgown. She lies in bed listening endlessly to tapes of John Denver or occasionally "Les Miserables."

I ride my bike through the woods. Take time each day to experience joy. Pray for peace and strength.

JULY 1990

Sometimes she's aware: "I didn't realize how many things I took for granted."

Sometimes she's in another world: "Get those barking dogs out of here!"

She's losing sense of time and place. The cancer has spread to her brain, my doctor explains.

She barely eats: a few teaspoons of yogurt, a half cup of water a day. How much longer? I come often to "Mommy-sit," as we tell her nine-year-old daughter. One day I sketch Donna sleeping. I'm trying to burn her image into my brain. I fantasize about the pillow on the bed and wonder if I could use it to end the suffering.

LATE JULY 1990

A sister flies in for the weekend. Miraculously, Donna rallies. She's awake and alert and conversing in real time.

"Is it possible? is there still hope?"

"No," my doctor answers quietly. "She's nearing the end. This is the time to say anything that still needs to be said."

But there's nothing left to say.

AUGUST 4, 1990, 10:30 A.M.

A serendipitous phone call home.

"Can't talk," my mother says. "She's having trouble breathing. I'm calling hospice."

I believe she waited for me. Minutes after I arrive, Donna, gasping for air, dies. As I stand crying, my mother holds me, patting my back. Then she leaves to tell my father. I sit alone on the bed, stroking Donna's arm. My father walks down the hallway and glances but can't come in.

Donna with her children, 1986

I feel the warmth gradually leave her hand, her arm, her shoulder, her neck. I touch her face.

She is wearing her birthday gift.

It's the first Shabbat in August. ❧

≋ Shaken

by Jonathan Markowitz

IT IS TUESDAY, SEPTEMBER 11, AND I am sitting in a conference room on the eighty-fifth floor of Tower One of the World Trade Center. The New York time is 8 A.M. and I have just phoned my family to wish them good morning and say that I'll be on the 4 P.M. flight.

I start to teach a seminar but am startled by a bang, like the sound and feel of two trains passing at high speed. I feel the building rock violently from side to side, look out the window, and see papers and office supplies strewn in the air like confetti during a ticker-tape parade. Seconds later the New York manager enters the conference room and calmly says he just watched an airplane hit the building. Immediately I am apprehensive for my staff and the people in the plane. However, the only action I can take is to dial 911, then grab my suitcase and leave the office with the rest of our staff.

We decide to take the B stairwell and begin to descend. I know we are in some danger but I try to joke around to keep everyone calm. Our office lease is up for renewal, and we were to have a meeting at 10 A.M. to discuss our alternatives. On the eightieth floor, I take a poll, and it is unanimously decided that we should look for new space.

On the seventy-seventh floor, we encounter a problem: A door somewhere below will not open. The people call out, and we find an open door higher up and exit into a hallway that is on fire. The scene is scary, surreal, but we are able to walk around the fire and continue to descend through another stairwell.

The descent is very hot and boring. All we do is go around and around. To ease the boredom and the fear we start to talk, help people who need assistance, and try not to slip on the stairs wet from water that is dripping and sloshing down from somewhere above.

Soon I hear, "To the right, to the right," and see the wounded descending. It is very sobering to see people in shock, soaked in blood. After they pass, we continue down, just a little more quietly.

As I approach the fiftieth floor, I see firemen on their way up. They look exhausted. They are climbing carrying a lot of heavy equipment. I overhear one fireman who is resting in a hallway complain of having chest pains. There are now two lines on the stairs: one going up and one coming down.

On the thirtieth floor, I come to a command center. Here a fireman asks to use my cell phone, and I say, "Sure," and hang around in hopes of getting more information. Also I figure that if he gets through, then I can call my wife and tell her I am okay. After a minute or two, the fireman, unable to reach anyone, gives me back my phone and tells me, "Go on down."

The rest of the descent goes pretty quickly. I enter the mezzanine area and see for the first time the burning wreckage in the courtyard. I avoid stopping to stare and head toward the center of the WTC.

I get as far as the Path train. Then I hear, "Everybody get down." I look over my shoulder and see a shock wave of dust and debris rushing toward me. I figure I have about four seconds. I look around and see a smoothie stand, lie down beside it, and wait for the cloud to envelop me.

All at once the lights go out, and I feel I cannot breathe because the dust is so thick and acrid. I reach into my suitcase and pull out my favorite shirt to use as a mask.

After a few minutes, I hear someone say, "Everyone be quiet and we will all get out." Another person instructs, "Everybody stand up and hold hands." A third person says, "I have a flashlight." I say, "I know where we are," and begin to call out landmarks as we walk toward an exit. Several minutes later we round a corner, climb some stairs, and emerge outside.

Dust and building pieces are everywhere. People are walking away from the WTC in shock. Down the block a restaurant employee is handing out water. I grab a cup, rinse out my mouth, and hand the cup

Jonathan Markowitz (2nd from left),
New York City, September 11, 2001
(Photo reprinted with permission from
AP /Wide World Photos)

to a colleague. I try my cell phone but can't get through to my family. And every phone booth I see has a long line. About twenty minutes later, when I reach the heart of Chinatown, I hear people screaming something about Tower One of the WTC collapsing. Finally, I find a print shop with a phone I can use. After several unsuccessful tries I reach my wife, assure her that I am not injured, and tell her I want to *bentsch Gomel* (recite the prayer of thanks for escaping danger).

On my way back to the hotel, the enormity of the day starts to sink in. I think about my wife Ruth, my kids, and my JRC community. I realize that many must not have survived.

Next I think about the humanity and cooperation of the people in the stairwells and around the WTC: how we worked together and helped each other so we could all survive.

However, Why, God? I feel my faith teetering. If this is a lesson, what are You trying to teach? Should I stop being Jewish?

These questions haunt me as I go to *minyan* the following Saturday. As we sing the morning blessings, I feel the pull of God on one side and my doubts on the other. The *Amidah* moves me more deeply than it ever has before. Yet I do not know whether to lose myself in prayer or to run out of the building.

During the closing meditations and prayers of the service, my doubts and my anger subside. A calm comes over me. I remind myself that I survived, that I am among friends. Admittedly, I don't have answers to what happened. But were I to give up my faith, then I would be the loser. ❧

◥ Exodus:
Crossing into the Second Half of Life
by Mel Patrell Furman

As much as we crave the comfort of featherbeds,
it eludes us. What with night sweats and reflux,
we are too anxious to be bound up in the bond of life,
struggling like flies amid its gossamer threads.
Like Jacob we are born to wrestle, and wrestle
we do, taking down the ordinary and going to the mat with routine.
The Red Sea rages through our wrists, knocks in our throats.
This is our legacy, like it or not: we must make this crossing or die.

Left–right: Rochelle M. Bernstein, Judy Mendel, Gail Brodsky,
Reggi Marder, and Ellen Gilbert, May 1997

We step into the sea, deadly tumultuous and wet
with the promise that routine will wash away
that slavery will dissolve like salt
that we will arrive not in heaven,
not in the *Goldeneh Medinah,*
but in a dried-out wasteland, the waiting room of wisdom,
studded with stones and broken only by little shrubs
yearning to speak to us, to burst into flame as we pass.
Here the signs of life are thirst and vipers,
and gleaming mirages of Egypt float on the hot sand,
where we wait for visions that may drive us to madness. ❧

🌊 OK, So I'm Old

by Anne Goldberg

I AM STANDING ON THE EL, LEANING against my backpack, and reading a novel to the rhythm of the swaying train car, when I hear a voice to my left: "Would you like to sit down?" Such an offer is a rarity on the el, so I look up to see who is making it. A young woman, maybe twenty years old, wearing a light blue jacket, is offering her seat to me.

To me?

Me?

This person is offering her seat to *ME?*

But you're supposed to offer your seat to an old person, not to me. I'm not old. I go to the gym twice a week. I take yoga. I even started hula lessons last Sunday!

Me?

I remember all the times my mother said, "You sit on my lap and let the lady sit down." (Acquiring good karma.)

I remember the evening I gave my place on the bus to an old man, and he passed it on to an even older woman who got on three stops later. (Sharing good karma.)

I remember offering a seat to a weary-looking woman on a Manhattan cross-town bus, and her saying, with great suspicion, "You don't have to do that."

"I know I don't have to," I told her, "but I want to. I'm on vacation and you've been at work all day." (Spreading good karma.)

Portrait quilt by Anne Goldberg, summer 2005

I look at the young woman who is waiting for my answer, and I wave aside her offer. "No, thanks, that's all right."

"Please," she insists, and stands up.

How many times have I done exactly that? How many times have I given my place to someone else and felt good in my soul for having done so? How can I say no to the young woman standing there, who is offering me this unwanted gift?

All that good karma comes crashing down on my head.

"Thank you." I smile at her and sit. ✒

❧ Saving Grandma's Candlesticks
by Roslyn Goodman Levinson

THE APPRAISER HELD ONE OF THE two tall, ornate silver candlesticks at eye level, turning it around. I sat across the table from him, eagerly anticipating his reaction. "Tell me about them," he said.

"They were my maternal grandmother's Shabbat candleholders," I said "She brought them from Europe as part of her dowry. She was just eighteen years old, betrothed to my grandfather, a man she'd never met, from her hometown in Lithuania."

"They're beautiful," the appraiser said. "Probably middle to late nineteenth century. You'd find a good auction market for them in New York—even better in Europe. They're worth at least $400. Do you plan to sell them?"

"Oh, no. They're a family heirloom. I wouldn't part with them, not ever. See how the silver is wearing off." I pointed to the edge of the square base of one where the metal beneath was beginning to show. "Should I have them re-silvered?"

"No. They're beautiful as they are. Keep them that way. Don't polish them with anything harsh. Silver polish will take more of the silver off. Just polish them with a jeweler's polishing cloth, and enjoy them." He added, "I'm glad you're keeping them." I was delighted with his approval.

Many years ago, when Grandma came to live with us after my father died, she brought only a few personal effects. Packed among her clothes were her two most prized possessions, her Shabbat

Roslyn Goodman (right) with her mother and grandmother, April 1942

candleholders and her hand-carved wooden clock, whose pendulum chimed the hour and half-hour. A little lady with silver-streaked black hair worn in a knot atop her head, she proudly placed the candlesticks on our dining room table and the clock on the mantle.

Every Friday, wearing an apron-covered housedress, Grandma would polish the silver until her candlesticks shone. At sundown she would light the candles in their holders, pass her hands above the flames, cover her eyes with her hands, and say the prayer ushering in the Sabbath. The candles would glow during dinner and throughout the evening, finally flickering and burning out at bedtime. To make sure they died out before we went to bed, Grandma would pare the candles down to the right size before lighting them. Blowing them out was forbidden.

I loved that ceremony. It gave me a feeling of peace, of love of family. Mother and I did dishes after the dinner Grandma had prepared. Often Grandma would make my favorite dish, *tzimmes,* her wonderful concoction of beef, carrots, sweet potatoes, onions, and lima beans sweetened with brown sugar. I would do her bidding all the next day so she could observe her day of rest.

Years later, when I was grown and about to marry, Grandma asked me if I would take care of her candlesticks when she died.

"Oh, yes, of course I will," I said.

"And will you light them on the Sabbath?"

"I will," I answered, "but I hope you'll possess them for a long time." I didn't want to think of her dying. I wanted Grandma in my life for many more years.

About one year after that conversation, I married. To my great disappointment my grandmother was too ill to attend Hal's and my wedding. She died several months later without telling her children who was to receive the few possessions she'd left. Fortunately, I'd told Mother about Grandma's and my conversation, and my promise to light her Shabbat candles.

When Mother and her oldest sister were packing Grandma's possessions, my aunt claimed Grandma's clock and the candlesticks. She thought those stately silver beauties would make handsome lamp bases.

"Oh, but Mother promised them to Roslyn," my mother exclaimed. "They had an agreement. Roslyn promised to light them on the Sabbath, so our mother told her she was to have them."

The candleholders have remained with me for fifty years. In our first apartment we had a gate-leg table that hugged the living room wall. Grandma's fourteen-inch-tall silver beauties stood regally on the dark wood table. When I remembered, I'd light them Fridays at sundown. When we moved into our new home, they glistened on the corner of my dining room buffet. I often forgot to light them on Friday evenings. There were too many distractions from my many activities and three active children, but I never failed to light them for Passover, Rosh Hashanah, and Yom Kippur. I kept them polished until they gleamed.

One evening at a party in my home, two antique-loving friends admired my candleholders, asking their origin. After explaining that they were part of Grandma's dowry, I added, "I saved them from becoming lamps."

Grandmother's candlesticks are precious to me, and I frequently think about my promise to her, which I regret I did not fulfill. My life, full with children and a career, rarely lent itself to the rituals of Shabbat. Now, in my senior years, my life is more routine. I light the Shabbat candles at sundown almost every Friday and savor the childhood memories this ritual brings. I visualize Grandma covering her eyes and beginning, *"Baruch atah adonay,"* after she strikes a match and lights the first candle. Remembering, I follow her lead. ❧

How I Stumbled onto the Sabbath and Came to Keep It in My Way

by Nina Raskin

For most of my life, Saturday was filled with activity. As a child I went to the local movie theater with my friends in the morning, and played in the park or in our Bronx apartment all afternoon. In high school I took modern dance lessons and art classes, and prepared for the big Saturday night date. As a young wife and mother, I devoted Saturday to looking for furniture, appliances, baby equipment, and a house. Later, as a clinical social worker, I worked on Saturday mornings and used the remainder of the day as a catch-all for domestic chores and everything else that I didn't have time for during the week.

Then, fifteen years ago, my mother died after a long illness and decline. Her last years were a source of anguish and grief. On the anniversary of her death, on a beautiful July evening, I lit a *yahrzeit* candle for the first time in my life. I placed the candle on our dining room table, in front of a window with the green expanse of the yard visible beyond it. Feelings of peace and beauty filled me, and I felt my mother's heart beating again. All night I awoke repeatedly to reassure myself that the candle's flame was still alive. For the next year I remembered that sense of my mother's presence, and the peace I had felt during the life of the *yahrzeit* candle.

The following year, my work was very difficult, and I would come home exhausted and troubled by a particular family I was working with. My efforts to protect a vulnerable child were failing, and I spent frustrating days in Juvenile Court. After one particularly wrenching Friday afternoon in court, I came home late. I sat looking out at the vista of fresh green trees and thought to myself, "I can experience the peace of my mother's *yahrzeit* every week." So we lit Shabbat candles, and Nat and I celebrated our first Shabbat.

At first he thought I was crazy, but he soon got into the spirit of it; and for the past dozen years or so, each week we have had a quiet Shabbat together. My work didn't get easier, but experiencing Shabbat gave me the energy to continue and was a way of honoring my mother and restoring her to me throughout the year. ❧

Marking the End of a Marriage: Let Me Count the Ways

by Susan P. Siebers

HOW MANY WAYS CAN THE END OF one marriage be finalized? For most Jews, it's one or possibly two: a civil divorce and perhaps a *get*. From my first marriage, however, I have not one, not two, but three divorces, and, incredibly, a Catholic annulment.

My first divorce was actually an Orthodox *get*, a formality which seemed to me to leave all future options open. Atypically, mine occurred before rather than after the civil divorce, since my soon-to-be ex-husband was leaving town before that court date. I realized that I was outside my normal realm when answering the rabbi's questions over the phone. I was asked if I ever use names other than Susan. Without thinking, I mentioned that when I read from the Torah, I use my Hebrew name, Sarah. This was back in 1980, when it was far less common for women to read from the Torah. There was silence at the other end of the phone; then the questions continued. When we walked into the room for the *get*, I had the feeling that all the rabbis were eying me with a "she's the one..." look.

In the Orthodox ritual, the man presents the *get* to the woman. So my only role was to accept it. The rabbis took me into consideration by asking, more than once, "Are you doing this of your own volition?" The *get* ceremony was interesting, but I felt detached from it. Being handed the *get* did not feel like the ending I needed.

My civil divorce went smoothly. Since I worked downtown, I simply took a slightly longer lunch so that I could do something special for myself upon leaving the courtroom. I had planned to celebrate by getting an ice cream cone and had enjoyed imagining what flavors I would order. To my disappointment, I discovered that since it was already fall, ice cream cones were no longer available. I settled for a nice piece of Marshall Field's chocolate and went back to work. But I still didn't have the closure I sought.

What finally satisfied my need to mark this life-cycle passage was a Reconstructionist *get*. This more egalitarian ceremony had me present the *get* as well as accept it. By this time, my ex-husband had moved out of state, so our JRC rabbi, Arnie Rachlis, stood in for him. That was a bit strange but okay with me, since it served my main need—namely, to participate actively in the ritual.

I thought I was done. One civil and two religious ceremonies should be enough for anyone. But some time later, my ex-husband contacted me to say that he was remarrying, that his future wife was Catholic, and that in order to be married in a Catholic ceremony, he needed an annulment of our marriage.

I found this puzzling, since he was Jewish and did not seem to want to renounce that part of himself. Friends of mine consulted their priest in Skokie, who also was mystified. The Archdiocese of Oklahoma was prepared to grant him an annulment whether or not I cooperated. My Catholic friends couldn't understand why I cared, or why I would participate in this. But I decided it was preferable for me to have my say. I did talk with a priest to find out more about the process and specifically how the church would view my son. The diocese's view was that after the annulment, my son would still be considered the offspring of a legitimate civil marriage, but that in its opinion, no religious marriage would ever have existed.

So I completed the questionnaire provided, answering such questions about the marriage as our state of mind entering into it, and why it had ended. All these many years later, I still don't really understand the process and wonder how my responses were viewed. But at any rate, the Catholic annulment was granted.

I have had more than enough of marital endings. Therefore, I am happy to report that my second marriage is now of long duration and I do not anticipate any more such endings. ❧

🌊 A Life Lesson

by Naomi Feldman

IT WAS APRIL, AND SCHOOL WAS OUT for a week. Dan and I had planned a vacation in California—our very first trip together—and we had worked hard to find the right locale, accommodations, and books to take along for what we hoped would be the start of many voyages of discovery together.

The first thing that went wrong was that it was cold. Very cold. The beaches of La Jolla were no place we wanted to be. Gone were our visions of lolling on the sand, enjoying the waves and the sunshine. So, ever hopeful, we went off to seek warmer climes in Palm Springs. If we ignored the too-rich looking kids cruising the main strip in their too-rich Cadillac convertibles, and if we ignored the hordes of shoppers cruising the stores searching for just one more thing to buy, it wasn't bad. But this was not our hoped-for idyll, either, so we left and found a rundown, once-chic hotel, occupied, it appeared, by one elderly man who swam laps every day in the pool, and by us. That suited us, and we were happy. So far, so good.

Five days later, we set out for the drive back to San Diego and the airport. We were halfway there when Dan said to me, "You've got the plane tickets, right?"

"No," I said, "you have them."

Clearly, neither of us had them. A telephone call back to the hotel produced no results: the tickets could not be found. At the airport we explained our problem to the agent, who told us that we would have to purchase new tickets, and that we might—underline "might"—get our money back if no one else showed up with our tickets. And so that's what we did.

What we realized on this trip was that in our former marriages, it was always the Other Spouse who was in charge of the plane tickets. So of course we each assumed that now, as then, the Other Person had them. Wrong. This was a classic example of what we should have known but did not: new relationships bring lots of baggage with them. In our case, since we were in our fifties, we were definitely not tabulae rasae. We had many years' worth of stuff: decades of dealing with someone else's foibles, whether how to spend a night out, or what to have for dinner, or how to store the coffee beans. These had all created patterns of behavior we were not even aware of: they were simply "how it's done." And here we were, embarking on a new chapter in heretofore separate lives, without a clue about the pitfalls of quotidian discoveries that lay ahead. The real moral of this tale is that one should assume nothing. Ever. ❧

◣ April 15, 2003

by Angela Allyn

Racing across town in the minivan
I ripped the first certifiable gray hair outta my head today.
Gray,
not blond
not golden,
ash gray.

A rite of passage barely noticed
packed in between a surprise three-hour managers' meeting
and the line at the post office
don't be late to the NEW carpool schedule (tag, you are it).

Oh, it's coming all right.
That doorway to another age is forming
in the haze of e-mails and junk mail and lots of appointments.
The weird menstrual cycle and shifting hormones and creaky
    stiff muscles are whispering:
    change.

And in the odd and heartbreaking way that my universe
    balances itself,
my nine-year-old daughter gets her first pimple
and suddenly needs to bathe—
she is entering the room I am about to leave.

So where are the drumming, the sage, the elders,
welcoming me to the third age?
I want my croning ceremony,
I want to mark this inevitable moment
with something more
than the mental note to pick up the henna that covers gray.

The cell phone rings,
the idiot driver in front of me makes a left turn from the right lane
and the river of life washes me on downstream.
My first gray hair blows out the window in the warm
    spring breeze.

For lunch tomorrow this newly minted crone
will get a pedicure,
and tonight, a fine red wine with the microwave dinner.
To celebrate my coming of age. ❧

🌊 This Body of Mine

by Angela Allyn

This body of mine is not the body I really wanted.
This skinshell is not the stuff of dreams
But it does the job.
Three other people have lived here
A House they were renting
While their own place was built
And we are still having
"Ownership Issues."
Squatters forget they don't own the place.

This body never got to be the body I envisioned—
Always more than I liked and less than I wanted
It would have been good to be 5'8 with smaller breasts
That wouldn't bounce then sag when I ran.
And the great bowl of my pelvis assured I would never have
A boyish dancer's body.

But in the end, the shell moves forward
Attempting to overcome any functional flaws.
The lack of a deep *plié*, a dearth of turn-out,
Completely pitiful extensions, and too long of a waist
      to grace a leotard—

How I managed to have a decade-long career as
   a professional dancer
With this jalopy of a carcass is a bloody miracle.

So I point my wagon down the long road of aging
Where the parts begin to fail.
My scars are chapter headings as questionable pieces are removed
For further study.
So far, none of my cellular improvisations has proved dangerous,
But it does put you on the lookout for unruly growth.

And I watch time passing in my structure
In my skin. ❧

❧ This Life Change

by Laurie Kahn

IT BEGAN ALMOST IMPERCEPTIBLY. Small lapses. I couldn't find my cup of coffee, and later a colleague emerged from the supply closet with it. Words and names disappeared when needed, resurfacing later. Was I sleep deprived or losing my mind or were my allergies acting up? I was in my mid-forties. My life was full, demanding, gratifying. Eventually, it occurred to me that these symptoms marked the beginning of menopause.

My initial response was to assault the bookshelves in search of guidance and wisdom. The first books I found must have been written by women granted sabbaticals from real life. These women went to yoga retreats, embraced the goddess, and were blessed with extensive knowledge of herbs, creams, and exotic treatments that allowed them to float through menopause. To them, hot flashes were power surges welcoming them into a time of transformation.

Then I found books with a more sobering tone. Early chapters described a stretch of time called peri-menopause, during which a woman would start noticing shifts in mood, changing patterns of menstruation, and so on. The authors listed symptoms and treatment options. Chapter headings included *Depression and Memory; Midlife Acne; Hormone Levels Are Only One Part of Your Libido; Marriage Goes Bankrupt; Menstrual Cramps and Pelvic Pain; Hair in the Wrong Places; Aids to Lubrication.* I began to experience these books the way that I imagine dogs experience humans talking at them: "Blah, blah, blah, your skin will dry up and blah, blah , blah you will lose your memory and maybe your mind, blah, blah, blah your vagina will dry up, blah, blah, blah your breasts will hurt, you will get fat, and you will be a shell of who you used to be and blah, blah . . ."

One by one, these books found their way into the garbage. Some were gently placed there, while others were hurled across the room, knocking over the table lamp.

I was surprised by how alone I felt. It's not that I had no friends. But my friends were younger or older, or their experiences differed from mine. I think there must be a women's lottery, and each woman gets a certain cluster of symptoms. My best friend had the "you-bleed-for-fourteen-days-a-month-and-become-anemic" cluster sprinkled with exhaustion, while I had the "turn-bright-red-at-staff-meetings-then-break-out-in-a-sweat" cluster sprinkled with momentary lapses where you can't remember the name of the client who has just told you her life story. My best friend and I would get together for weekly lunches. She'd be wearing long sleeves, a sweater, and a jacket, while I would show up in a sleeveless shirt. We were living in different thermal realities.

As my desperation and isolation grew, I would try to spot women approaching fifty in the ladies' room. I found myself wanting to politely ask, "How is your vagina doing?" or "Have you recently forgotten the name, or even worse, the plot, of a book you just finished?" I tried to restrain myself, fearing I might be reported for some form of peri-menopausal harassment.

As the months passed, I was becoming sleep deprived, and I felt in a constant state of PMS. Sex was losing its appeal. I turned to my husband for help

"Honey, I think I'm losing my mind," I would whisper as we were falling asleep.

"I spent twenty-five minutes looking for my car today because I couldn't remember where I parked it." He would gently pat me on the head.

Some nights a layer of sweat would wake me up, and I'd nudge my husband and ask him to feel the moisture on my body. I thought a witness might help to assure me I wasn't imagining what was happening. He would be cooperative and quite pleasant, considering I had woken him up from a deep sleep.

"Yes, you are kind of damp," he would agree, then turn over and go back to sleep. He never complained about the air conditioner set at fifty-five degrees, or about the noise of the fans that I put at either end of our bed. His gentle yet patronizing responses inspired me, however, to consider a more dramatic approach.

"I am living in someone else's body, and the body I previously inhabited is missing," I told him. This time he looked a bit alarmed, but managed to smile with that "You'll be OK" look on his face. I was disappointed.

I was desperate to evoke some empathy for this major earthquake in my body. One night I asked him how he would feel if he found out that part of aging was that his penis would slowly wither and then fall off. For a moment the pupils of his eyes got bigger. I thought I had finally grabbed his attention.

He took a deep breath. "I'm sorry you're having such a difficult time," he sympathized, then went to check his e-mail.

Unlike other dramatic life changes familiar to women, there is nothing romantic about menopause. Pregnancy, that wonderful, miraculous state of being, is met with adoring glances, gentle pats on the belly, and a universe that opens doors for you and offers to lift your heavy packages. Not so with the midlife bulge that accompanies these later hormonal changes, your enlarged belly peeking out from an over-sized shirt. At best people pretend not to notice.

I would like to tell you about the peace that came from the acceptance of this life change. I reluctantly admit to taking vitamins called "Menopoise" and using an occasional cream that promises to ease the signs of aging. I look in the mirror and notice the footprints of aging on various parts of my face and body. I have not experienced the promised power surges of wisdom, but I do now walk in the world with the confidence and competence that comes from age, or maybe perseverance. In the midst of occasional despair, it does not escape me that I am blessed and that change is part of the journey. ✒

I'm Sean Connery

by Syd Lieberman

SOMETIMES YOU'RE IN THE RIGHT place at the right time, and you get a once-in-a-lifetime opportunity. One such windfall happened to me outside an ice cream parlor in my hometown of Evanston, Illinois. But to understand the significance of this moment, you have to understand something about me.

Much of my idea of what it means to be a man has come from the movies. When I was younger, my three role models were Marlon Brando, Paul Newman, and Humphrey Bogart. What movies! What characters! What lines!

Brando as the sweaty Stanley in *A Streetcar Named Desire*, standing on the pavement, shouting: "Stella! Stella!" Or playing ex-boxer Terry Malone in *On the Waterfront*, explaining to his brother why he shouldn't have asked him to throw the biggest fight of his life. "Charlie, Charlie. No . . . No . . . Wow . . . You don't understand. I could have had class. I could have been a contender. I could have been somebody, instead of a bum, which is what I am. Let's face it."

Or Paul Newman, with his blue-eyed, pouty good looks, in *Cool Hand Luke*, standing up to the evil prison warden, who says of Newman's resistance, "What we have here is a failure to communicate." Newman just smirks in reply.

Or Bogart in *Casablanca* standing in a foggy airport, making sure that Ingrid Bergman and her husband get on the plane to Lisbon.

Bergman would have stayed in Casablanca, but her husband is a world-famous resistance fighter who wouldn't be able to go on without her. Bogart and Bergman had had a whirlwind affair in Paris, but he now gives up the love of his life, because he knows what's best for her, her husband, and the world. He says, "It doesn't take much to see that the problems of three little people don't amount to a hill of beans in this crazy world. . . . We'll always have Paris." And then he chucks her under the chin and says what he always would say in their city: "Here's looking at you, kid."

You would think that when you get older, the desire to be a sexy, tough leading man would disappear. What actually disappeared was me. When I was young, sometimes as I walked along the street I would engage in a little innocent flirting. I would check out a girl or discover that she was checking me out. Every now and then our eyes would meet and we would smile.

But now no one looks at me as I walk down the street. I've become invisible. If I glance at a girl and she notices, she gives me a mean stare as if I were a dirty old man. When people do see me, all that registers is bald head and gray fringe, and they want to offer me a seat on the subway.

So who could be my new role model? Bogart died of lung cancer a long time ago. Newman's selling salad dressing. And even though Brando churned out memorable tough-guy lines until he died—"I gave him an offer he couldn't refuse"—who would have wanted to look like him? There's only one way to describe the change from slim to bloated, and that's using his own line from *Apocalypse Now:* "The horror."

But then I found my role model: Sean Connery. Even though I'm not 6´2″ or Scottish, I look a little like him. Bald, gray fringe, white beard with a little brown reaching up around the chin. And he's perfect. When he was younger, he played Agent 007 with sophisticated machismo: "I'm Bond. James Bond." His best performance was as a stand-up guy, the Irish cop who helped Kevin Costner take on the mob in *The Untouchables*. And as an older man, he still plays the romantic lead in adventure films, and he still wins the girl.

Connery was knighted in 2000, but who cares about that? In 1989 when he was nearly sixty—I just turned sixty myself last April—a *People Magazine* poll named him the sexiest man alive!

One day he appeared on TV in an American Express ad. At the end, as they typed his name on the card, he said "I'm Sean Connery."

I loved this line. "I'm Sean Connery." I began to say it all the time. It became my mantra. I'd enter a room and wait for Adrienne to look up so I could say "I'm Sean Connery." I'd sit down to dinner and say, "I'm Sean Connery." I'd get into bed with Adrienne and smile, "I'm Sean Connery." I liked saying it. I liked feeling it. "I'm Sean Connery."

Then my magical moment happened. Adrienne and I were sitting and licking ice cream cones outside our neighborhood ice cream parlor when two young girls walked by. One stopped. Her eyes got really big and her mouth fell open. She stood there staring, and finally she asked, "Are you Roger Moore?

It was an honest mistake—Moore played James Bond after Connery. But, even better, it was the perfect mistake. Against all odds, it provided me with my cue. It was as if I had been practicing for this very moment. Her question gave me a once-in-a-lifetime opportunity to say "I'm Sean Connery," and have someone actually believe it.

I looked up, smiled politely, and said. . . .

"No."

No? No! I had flubbed a once-in-a-lifetime opportunity. Adrienne stared at me in disbelief. I've been kicking myself and she's been teasing me about it ever since.

Now some people say that in this lifetime you need to grab an opportunity when it comes your way because you don't get a second chance. But that's not always true, especially if you're a storyteller.

So now you probably know what I want you to do. When you meet me, please humor me by asking, "Are you Roger Moore?"

If you do, you'll get to hear me say my best, most polished line: "No . . . I'm Sean Connery." ∿

Syd Lieberman, 2000

❧ A Jewish Year on the Path toward Healing and Wholeness

by Linda Mathias Kaskel

As an adolescent, I often participated in so-called theater games. In one activity, we would all steady ourselves and prepare for one of us to fall back into the arms of the rest of the group. When it was my turn to fall, I would hesitate for fear that no one would catch me.

In 2002, the week before the High Holidays, I discovered a lump. I performed most of my pre–Rosh Hashanah activities as a mindless robot shuffling between scans, probes, and tests. For ten days the question of who would live or die was my shocking personal reality. The night before I went into the hospital for the tumor removal and biopsy, I stood in the *sukkah*. As the wind shook the structure, I felt chilled by my own vulnerability. And yet, I thought, if this flimsy structure can survive the storms it faces, so can I. From deep inside arose prayers for strength, courage, and hope. I entered the hospital expecting the tumor to be benign and planning to resume my hectic routine the next day.

The first thirty-six hours in the hospital are a blur. I awoke to the rhythm of machines, my body wrapped in yards of tubes. The surgery had taken much longer than originally expected, as lymph glands had to be removed. The following day, the surgeon stood over my bed. The phrases *going home, chemotherapy, radiation,* and *side effects* repeatedly left his mouth. What was he talking about? None of these words made sense to me. I was in shock.

Later that evening, as I lay alone in the dark, the news began to sink in. Fear seemed to empty me of all strength. How would I be able to leave this bed and face the long journey ahead? I would not be going home in time for *Simchat Torah* services. I would not be dancing with the Torah or celebrating to the sound of *klezmer* music. I cried and tossed and turned with worry.

Several days later, tubes removed, I returned home to focus on my healing. I set out on a frantic search for the optimum medical treatment and a large dose of spiritual medicine. Soon, friends and cancer survivors were calling, offering me encouragement and information. At first I fought all the options. But my research told me that prayer and chemotherapy were the necessary first steps.

Twenty days into chemotherapy, the trees were shedding the last of their leaves, and the earth was becoming dormant for winter. I began losing my hair and my energy. I managed the other side effects with modern medicine and shaved my to-do list to top priorities only. Deep down I remained scared about the unknown. A community of support emerged: empathic family and friends bearing chicken soup and humor. I was no longer alone on the path toward healing.

In the darkest and coldest season of the year, we celebrated Hanukkah. Lighting the candles reminded all of us to celebrate with optimism and re-dedication, even in the middle of worry and gloom. I focused on light, warmth, and new beginnings. One-third of the way through chemo, I had learned to do less and appreciate more.

I completed chemotherapy as the first spring bulbs were appearing. With a new sense of lightness and energy, I planned our family's annual Seder. As a family we joyfully recited the *Shehekheyanu*, blessing another opportunity to be together. We dipped the new spring greens into salt water and acknowledged that tears of joy—and of sorrow—often accompany new beginnings.

Around the next bend in the healing path, daily radiation treatments loomed. I am good at organizing and planning, but I was overwhelmed by the task of creating a space in my life for this. The treatment would be at the same time each day for almost two months, but the side effects were unpredictable. My body responded to the treatment with intense exhaustion, as if a two-ton weight had been attached to each limb. While the sun shone outside, inside the gloom and sadness reappeared. I was angry! Healing was not supposed to be this hard. Once again, friends and healers rallied around me with offers of help and broad shoulders to lean on.

Radiation therapy ended as my daughter graduated from high school. We took the time to acknowledge the victories with prayers of thanksgiving and celebration amid our community of helpers. Early in the treatment process, we had decided to celebrate each small milestone. I set my sights on daily blessings, avoiding the worries about if or when the cancer would return.

The following year, as a cancer survivor, I prepared for the Days of Awe with renewed energy and faith. Like the sounds of the *shofar* service, I began whole, was broken into small pieces, and returned whole again. In the process, I have challenged my adolescent fear of entrusting my life to other people. I closed my eyes and fell backwards into the arms of medical and spiritual healers. As I journeyed toward healing, I felt like Dorothy moving along the yellow brick road: I discovered that most of what I sought had actually been there all the time. Physically, I am learning to appreciate the healthy cells throughout my body, and to accept the effects of treatment. Emotionally, I am reminded not to spend too much time worrying about the future but rather to focus on the internal strength that accompanies courage and hope. Communally, I am so grateful to be living among a caring and supportive collective of family and friends. Over the past year I have learned firsthand that healing is not a cure of disease but an ongoing process of small victories in the lifelong struggle for wholeness of soul, mind, and body. ◞

~ You're Wearing Three Socks!

by Beverly Friend

TODAY, DAVID IS WEARING THREE socks, two on one foot. Yesterday, he wore only two, but they were on the same foot.

Sometimes he puts on underwear.

Sometimes not.

Occasionally, when reminded, he dons the underwear over his outer clothing.

He doesn't care.

Unfortunately, I do.

I've known David since 1957 in my first single life as a Northwestern University graduate student. I dated him. Betty, my roommate, dated him. Eventually we all married other people.

He was a good choice for a playmate but not for a husband. David never wanted children, and he was a maverick. Outspoken, stubborn, opinionated, and bright as a shiny new dime, David was the first of our crowd to earn a Ph.D. and the first to teach on the college level.

While he remained on the periphery of my life—invited to birthdays, my daughters' Bat Mitzvahs, and other celebrations—it wasn't until my husband Jim died in 1987 that David took on a more significant role. By that time, he had been divorced for several years; though if you asked him today, he would insist he was still married, that his wife lives in our city, and that he sees her on occasion.

About a year after my husband's death, we began to see each other more regularly. In 1996, when I bought a condo, he moved in with me. I didn't need a husband but was happy to have him as a playmate as the golden years approached.

Yes, he was odd, but he'd always been odd. Yes, he was forgetful, but who isn't as we grow older? It wasn't until his 1997 heart attack and bypass surgery that I was able to get David to seek sufficient medical attention to diagnose him with early Alzheimer's. His mother had also been a victim of the illness.

I had always thought Alzheimer's was a disease of forgetting, but it is far more than that. David gradually became unable to sequence activities. I had never realized how the simplest of activities requires sequencing:

Take a bowl from the cupboard.

Take the Raisin Bran, his favorite cereal, from another cupboard.

Pour cereal into the bowl.

Take milk from the refrigerator.

Pour milk into the bowl.

Return milk to the refrigerator.

Get a spoon from the drawer.

Take the bowl to the kitchen table.

Sit down and eat.

David skipped more and more of the steps, until I realized that he was beginning to choke on cereal that he was eating dry.

He has lost his executive ability. That's the official term for being able to carry through an activity. My vocabulary is expanding. I now know about catastrophic moments, verbal cueing, and geriatric psychiatry; and I have learned that the Alzheimer's patient is always right, because his reality is as genuine to him as mine is to me.

I have also learned the value of support groups as his behavior became more and more bizarre, his abilities more and more limited. He can no longer tell time or make a phone call. He can name only two animals when the doctor asks him to cite as many as he can recall in one minute.

I thought I had solved all of our ever-increasing problems by hiring a male caregiver to live with us, a vibrant forty-two-year-old hale and

David and Beverly in Hawaii during happier times

hearty Russian. However, since then, David has fled four times, twice when on outings and twice from the house. I met several helpful Niles, Skokie, and Lincolnwood police officers as they returned him.

We entered a new, sad phase of our lives when I placed David in the Alzheimer's unit of Belmont Village in Glenview. Day One, the day of placement, was from Hell as he shouted out about being held against his will and being unable to make his own choices.

Fascinatingly, whenever he's really distressed, he not only threatens loudly to sue, but also calls out the name of Congresswoman Jan Schakowsky as a mantra that might channel his salvation. "I will call Jan Schakowsky," he'll cry out. "She'll take care of this. You'll see!" I wonder what she would say if she were to learn of this surprising consequence of her work on behalf of the elderly.

Day Two was a study in contrasts. David meekly accompanied me across the hall from his room to dance with the other residents, and then we left the locked unit to attend a wine-and-cheese party. He asked no questions, not even "Where am I?" or "Why am I here?" We returned to his room and watched "Jeopardy" on TV, as we were wont to do at home, and then, when he fell asleep, I kissed him on the forehead and tiptoed out.

I planned to wait at least a month before daring to take him entirely out of the building, lest he dig in his heels and trigger a catastrophic moment by refusing to return. I haven't as yet needed to call in a geriatric psychiatrist, and I hope not to. But I am learning this lesson: "The only thing to expect is the unexpected."

In the past six months, we've met and mastered many hurdles. David has come out of the home for short forays, mostly for appointments with physicians. For a longer family adventure, such as Passover or my mother's one-hundredth birthday party, I arrange a driver and pal to accompany him.

While I worry and fret and make plans, David lives in an eternal present. With the past unremembered and the future inconceivable, all we really have is the present moment to savor fully. I am trying to live this way, too. And that may be the biggest lesson of all. ❧

❧ My Great, Good Friend Sam

by Eileen Heisler

IN EARLY 1980 SAM AND I BECAME co-workers. We would soon become
fast, true friends.

Sam was a Renaissance guy with huge appetites and even huger
generosity. With no wife or children to siphon off his energies, and his
sisters and extended family living out of town, Sam spared nothing for
his friends. He lavished us with gifts and feasts, hosted antique hunts,
and acquainted us with nationally renowned artists.

Whatever Sam did, he did with his own brand of panache. For
example, Sam had three season tickets to the symphony. It was his
dearest pleasure to invite a couple of friends to each concert.

Sam also believed that if there was a reason to collect something,
it must be done ardently and thoroughly. And so he did: hundreds
of rare art books; pottery of every size and shape; cookbooks and
kitchen utensils; and countless LP records, eventually replaced with
high-quality Phillips CDs. Plus paintings, kaleidoscopes, hats, green
Depression glass, and antique chocolate candy molds. A practical
person might ask: where does anybody put so much stuff?

In Sam's house, our Jewish household learned to make Christmas
cookies. For many years he hosted five families of co-workers, with
spouses and children, for an eight-hour day of cookie baking in
early December. It was common to run to his second refrigerator for
replenishments of the twenty-five pounds of butter. And of course

Christmas cookie baking with Sam (white shirt), c. 1990

there were several ten-pound sacks of flour and more chocolate chips and sprinkles and frosting than an institutional bakery. The only house rule: we had to use Sam's special recipes. The hundreds of cookies we baked were destined to come into the office for day after day of feasting from mid-December through Christmas.

When Sam made fudge, it was the delight of the office. He would make sure that everyone knew when he'd made an eight- to ten-pound batch, with and without nuts, of course.

It probably won't surprise you to learn that when Sam went to the Fannie May factory outlet, he needed help getting the bundles to the car. It was a good thing he had a second freezer for all the candy. When the staff at the Paulina Meat Market saw Sam coming, they hurriedly checked the back stock room.

One afternoon, we overheard Sam making his annual doctor's appointment. He told several of us that he would fool the doctor one more time. I remember him giggling with the planned deception. Sam thought he was borderline diabetic. His sure-fire plan was once again to stay off sugars for forty-eight hours and come through the tests with flying colors. After this visit Sam admitted with some delight that the doctor had guessed his modus operandi and warned him of the damage he was doing to his eyesight and circulation.

Eventually Sam was forced to move to Nashville to be cared for by his sister. By then diabetes had cost him his legs and his eyesight.

Near the end, I was too much the coward to fly to Nashville. We spoke on the phone several times, sharing happy memories. He asked what mementos we wanted from his vast collections, and we negotiated over shipping a few things. Wanting to keep him preoccupied, I asked him to search his vast collection for several obscure Vivaldi CDs. We debated whether he had them on records or on new CDs. It turned out that he was able to find several, and searching for them did the trick: it kept him busy.

I was away when Sam's sister called to tell us he'd died peacefully in his sleep, of kidney failure. He had refused dialysis. His sister said that, till the end, Sam had been happily preoccupied with sharing his collections and shipping things to friends. He'd also come into a few dollars in his final days, so he'd gone into town on a final shopping and eating spree. She said his closest friends would understand. And we do. ❧

❧ Simple Pleasures

by Adrienne Lieberman

MY MOTHER WAS DIFFICULT TO PLEASE. None of her four children
ever thought we got it right: my sister who made her a grandmother at
forty-four, then returned to garner bachelor's and master's degrees;
I who married my high school sweetheart instead of the wealthy,
exotic Easterner I might have captivated in college; my two smart,
hard-working brothers.

In recent years, my mother has become easy to please. But that's
only because this woman, who once inflicted on us the plots of every
movie and book she encountered, who read Shakespeare and loved
the opera, and who relentlessly chronicled our funny childhood
sayings and her far-flung travels, can no longer remember her name.
"Your guess is as good as mine," she blithely told the nurse who had
asked her that most basic question.

Thanksgiving at my house, her last time, she heard Zach's
girlfriend play the violin, then afterwards—having already forgotten
why—hummed Massenet's poignant *Elegy* all the way home. A year
and a half ago, her participation in our family Seders ended even
more abruptly. For the first half of her last Seder, Mom had joined
in the singing, and we all imagined that some good years lay ahead.
But when my sister Phyllis left to serve the dinner, Mom no longer
recognized anyone else at her end of the table. It was then that she
finally slipped her moorings in time and wondered tearfully whether

Emma and her great-grandmother, summer 2004

her father—forty years dead and never much caring about her whereabouts when he was alive—knew where she was. I reassured only myself by telling her that everyone who needed to know where she was knew. Everyone, of course, but her.

My mother, who unwittingly taught me to be a grudge collector, now sets a new example by leaving her own considerable grudges in the shadows. She accepts my help so sweetly, I gleefully unwrap the long-overdue gift of her unalloyed pleasure. Another nugget came a half-century late to assuage my child's hunger, but I had to laugh at its sheer guilelessness. "You can't be Adrienne," she argued, when I introduced myself to her.

"Why not?" I asked.

Her answer: "Adrienne's pretty."

My mother's descent into forgetfulness has turned her children into the indulgent parents she and we always craved. And now we watch her navigate the mirror-image path of a baby. On a late summer day,

Phyllis and I brought Mom's eleven-month-old great-granddaughter Emma for a visit to the nursing home. Emma and my mother were both wearing salmon pink pants of the pull-up, washable variety. We wheeled them to the outside garden, Emma in her stroller and Mom in her wheelchair. Phyllis sat Emma on a picnic table, and, as Emma pinched her Cheerios and teased us each in turn by appearing to offer us one, then eating it herself, we soaked in the dappled sunshine. Soon Emma warmed up enough to play patty-cakes and peek-a-boo with each of us in turn. Mom joined in, loudly reciting patty cakes and even doing peek-a-boo herself, then chortling at Emma's response. Like Emma, Mom repeatedly made tentative motions to get out of her chair, lifting her feet off the footrest and attempting to plant them on the ground. But for Emma, walking was imminent. Mom's walking days have retreated into an ever more distant past. One bright summer day, turning to fall, their trajectories intersected for a moment. And for that moment I felt the fierce pleasure of life's fleeting passage with the grateful simplicity of a child. ✺

Becoming Strangers

by Rochelle M. Bernstein

I HAD ALWAYS LOVED MY PARENTS' bedroom set. Each piece of furniture curved and swooped along its length. The wood was patterned and inlaid. Art deco.

The armoire was an Aladdin's cave of wonders. Two long doors on either side opened to cedar-lined closets. The right one held my mother's sheared beaver coat. I took every opportunity to open the door, smell the cedar, and swathe myself in the deep brown softness.

In the middle, above the three curving bottom drawers and below the very top drawer too high for me to reach, was the secretary. It had a drop-leaf desk, cubbyholes, and tiny drawers that drew me back most often. One small drawer revealed a pair of ebony castanets. Tucked toward the back on the right, a Zulu dagger with a short curved blade sat in an ominous black sheath. Both were souvenirs of my father's wartime travels.

When we brought Mom to live with us in Chicago, the entire bedroom suite, save this piece, fit in her room. With no space in any other room large enough, we had to find it another home. Our next-door neighbors solved our problem, and I began to remove and sort the contents before they took it in.

Among all the things I knew by heart, tucked under the suspended cubbies and drawers, I found a small cigar box I had never seen. Inside I found pictures of my father taken during the war. Some were of him alone; others showed him with shipmates. I suspected he'd sent these to my mother. A small folded envelope held pictures of my mother. I suspected he'd carried these with him.

One picture struck me so, I felt almost embarrassed looking at it. It was not a picture of my mother, that is, not a picture intended for one's child. Caught in an unguarded moment, my mother looks out of it at a husband she misses very much. Her hair, combed in a pompadour at the front, hangs loose at the back of her neck. Her expression is relaxed, sultry. I remembered having seen something of that look several years earlier.

I'd arrived in Philadelphia in the afternoon. The flight had been tedious, crowded, and late. I needed to get to sleep. Every six weeks for months I'd been making these weekend visits to get Mom to doctors, Doppler studies, EEGs, EKGs, MRIs, and all the other diagnostic appointments that nevertheless failed to save us from the diagnosis of Alzheimer's disease.

Mom and I had been sitting in the living room watching television, which provided the room's only light. I got up from my father's old chair and gently nudged her awake. "It's time to go to bed, Mom." Then I went into the kitchen to close the door to the basement, so she wouldn't inadvertently tumble down the stairs. By the time I got back to the living room, my mother had begun to rouse herself. I turned from fastening the front door latch to see her walking toward me, smiling. I'd never seen that smile before.

It had none of the levels of intimacy and experience that build between a mother and daughter over the years of growing together and apart and together again. None of the "here we are again, and isn't it odd and remarkable that we should be here together" qualities that levitate the corners of the mouth and crinkle the corners of the eyes just so. Before I could react, my mother came up to me. She placed her left hand on my forearm and said, still smiling, "I'm so pleased to have met you. I hope I'll see you again soon." And with that, she turned to go up the stairs to bed.

I stood there transfixed by two totally different experiences. The first was shock, as a large piece of steel lodged just below my heart and rampaged into my stomach and other vital organs. As the knifing cold spread, I thought, "She doesn't know me." My mother stood warming me with a smile, yet she hadn't a clue who I was. It was as strange as suddenly finding myself on the dark side of the moon.

The second experience, however, had the flavor of nostalgia. Suddenly, in the most wrenching circumstance, I realized that I'd been given an extraordinary opportunity: to see my mother as others might have known her. As my father had known her.

The Esther Bernstein I knew was a painfully shy and self-critical woman. In spite of this shyness, or perhaps because of it, she had always made others feel at home. Her fan club extended from my father's entire family to his war buddies, the frat boys from Rho Pi Phi whom she commandeered into making potato *latkes* in her restaurant kitchen one Sunday morning, and every person I ever introduced to her.

Here she was, in the moment, a woman of great charm and warmth. My mother, who in her "right mind" believed herself anything but charming and attractive, had been liberated from her self-consciousness by some dreadful genetic catastrophe. She'd slipped out of reality so gracefully, I could almost hear the tinkle of ice in a highball glass. Whatever party she was leaving with a becoming reluctance, she couldn't leave without saying goodnight to her daughter, the stranger.

On an evening visit to the nursing home to which we reluctantly gave her, I got off the elevator opposite the nurses' station. There was my mother, in her robe and slippers, feet on the desk and chair tipped back. Her arms were crossed, her eyes smiling. The nurses were laughing. My mother turned toward me. "And just what can we do for you this evening?"

That cold sensation never went away completely; I just learned to live around it. I stood dumb in the silence somewhere between "Come back" and "Hello." I was one stranger among many, loving her again and again as she became so essentially, improbably, herself. So pleased to have met her, and hoping to see her again. ❧

⌘ One Life for Another

by Carol Neubauer Friedman

in memory of Lawrence Jack Levinson
January 24, 1911–January 29, 2003

"I ASKED HIM TO TAKE MY LIFE AND give Rick his," he rasped through his scratchy throat, parched by encroaching dehydration. Long gone were the years when Grandpa Larry hauled the week's groceries up four flights of stairs to set a Shabbat table for three generations of family and a few widows from his apartment building in Skokie. Gone were the days when he shopped for his sisters–in-law and hand-delivered their medications and groceries, or drove them to doctors' appointments. Gone were the days when Grandpa stretched uncomfortably on the carpeted floor of his den to build Lincoln Log houses to his great-grandsons' exact specifications.

"It doesn't work that way, Grandpa!" I blinked back tears as I stared at his bent body folded into the upholstered chair. At 92, his body was surrendering to the battles he had been fighting for more than half his life; pain had surreptitiously moved in and become a full-time resident. Although Grandpa didn't really believe in God in a traditional sense, he was willing to barter his life for his grandson's. Somehow, in his way of looking at the world, it was one or the other, and as weary as he was, Grandpa was good for one last deal with the divine. He was good.

Several weeks later, our three young sons hunkered against yet another hospital wall, so accustomed to hospitals that they might have been practicing a tornado or terrorist drill in their school's musty basement. In the three months since their father's near-fatal bicycle accident, their once-familiar sense of the way things work or should work had become a threadbare blanket of raveling holes, hung out for sale in the foreign market of their disquieting dreams. Across town, Rick labored unconsciously to stitch frayed neuron to neuron, fumbling for the next thread of life, while our children, no longer innocent, waited to step inside the quiet hospital room for what I suspected would be their last visit with their beloved great-grandfather.

"You're part of my family now," he croaked when my turn finally came. I sat silently at his raised bedside stroking his smooth hand, now unencumbered by IVs and tape. "Don't be sad. This isn't sad. It's what I wanted, what I asked for. Remember? Remember that!"

Eight months later, Yom Kippur dawn quietly filled our home. On this day off from the usual mad dash to bus stops and homerooms, Rick and I took a moment to remember Grandpa. My warm hand stroked his whiskery cheek as tears silently washed away the crusty sleep from our eyes.

"Remember the story of the *Lamed-Vavniks*, Rick?"

Years before, Rick and I had sat together on the crumbling steps of the old Portuguese synagogue in Amsterdam, wondering if our future would include a life together. We talked about our vision of the world and what we had heard about the *Lamed-Vavniks,* the thirty-six righteous people who at any given time wander the world, unaware of their status and unrecognized by others. They do what they can, in their humble, unassuming way, to offset evil and suffering with their own good deeds. The key, we had learned, is that they live anonymously. When one dies, another joins the ranks of the *Lamed-Vavniks,* because it takes no more and no less than thirty-six of these selfless individuals to temper the injustice and misfortune in the world.

"Maybe Grandpa was one of them. You know, after the accident, Grandpa asked God to take his life and give you yours." Rick had never heard the story of Grandpa's bargain. "Maybe that's what happened." Tears choked back words. He rolled his head restlessly on the flattened pillow, crushed by the weight of another sleepless night. Did he want me to continue?

Grandpa and his grandsons, Gabriel, Aaron, and Daniel Friedman, 2001

"Maybe that was his final act of righteousness. Maybe that's what it took finally to release him from his constant pain and start you on your way back to us." In a strange way, grounded in their physical and emotional resemblance, he actually seemed to have been reborn into his grandfather's bodily shape, his form suddenly aged and bent by the terrible time-machine of trauma. There had, indeed, been some kind of mystical switch, some kind of undefined redemption: not a miraculous release, but a further journeying.

"Every time I look at you, I see him." Grandma's pure white hair bobbed atop her bent shoulders as she leaned over his wheelchair stretching her crooked arm across Rick's hunched back as they gazed peacefully at the newly unveiled grave. I knew I was not the only one who had noticed the transformation—the way Grandpa had quietly left a space for Rick to reclaim. Indeed, every time Rick rocks himself from seated position to standing or shuffles unevenly into a room, I see Grandpa in my mind's eye. Grandpa's last bargain with God offered one life for another. ❧

～ Waking to My Grandmother's Hands

by Kim Moldofsky

Two weeks ago I awoke to my grandmother's hands. It wasn't her gentle caress rousing me from sleep; rather, it seemed that her stiff, arthritic hands had somehow replaced mine in the night. It was like the movie *Freaky Friday*, in which a teenager and her middle-aged mom mysteriously switch bodies, except I'm thirty-five and my nana passed away at seventy-two. Like a curious infant I stared at my hands as I wiggled my unfamiliar digits. Where did these come from? How do they work?

Nearly a decade ago I was diagnosed with Sjögren's syndrome (SS), an autoimmune dysfunction in which the immune system attacks the body's moisture-producing glands, the ones that make tears and saliva. SS is often found in conjunction with more complex autoimmune diseases like lupus or rheumatoid arthritis. Although the diagnostic blood tests that revealed my illness included a sky-high rheumatoid factor, I initially had no arthritic symptoms.

My paternal grandmother developed rheumatoid arthritis in her thirties, and I have a maternal cousin with multiple autoimmune illnesses. Rather than a typical biological clock, I have more of an autoimmune alarm clock. My SS is fairly stable and manageable. My eyes are too dry for contact lenses, and I must drink water in order to speak clearly and swallow food, but these are nuisances, not disabilities. For the most part, I've been able to hit the snooze

Photo by Laura Friedlander

button and continue on. I lead an active life with my busy family. For nearly two years I've been exercising regularly, including twice-weekly karate training. In fact, I'm in the best shape of my life, so it was a bit surprising when my buzzing autoimmune clock awoke me to a new reality.

With two young children, I tend to opt for phone consultations when problems arise. The fact that I showed up in his office probably revealed more than any blood test could. Fortunately, Dr. F. did not give me the gloom-and-doom prognosis I feared. He showed concern, ordered diagnostics, and gave me permission to tell my husband when I needed a nap or extra help without feeling like I was simply being lazy. He encouraged me to continue the routines of my life as best I could, including my karate.

Karate training strengthens my body, focuses my mind, and builds my spirit. It's something I hope to continue for many years. "Just don't go breaking four-inch boards," he joked. I assured him that in all my training time, I'd never seen boards at my *dojo* (training hall).

To my surprise, the following week my karate *sensei* presented me with a board. It was less than an inch thick, so I wouldn't be going against doctor's orders if I tried to break it. Kick-crash-smash! I did it!

The broken board pieces now decorate my bedroom wall. On one half I glued a circa-1990 Nike ad. It reads: *You are not destined to become the women who came before you! So if you inherit something, inherit their strength, inherit their resilience. Because the only person you are destined to become is the person you decide to be.*

Those pieces are a reminder of my own strength—strength I never imagined I had. When I read the quote, I think about my grandmother and begin to see her as a strong woman who put aside her pain to raise two boys, and who lived long enough to know all of her grandchildren. Rather than view my cousin as a victim of her own body, I think of her as one who endures, a strong-willed wife and mother of three with a successful career. I reframe my own health problems, too; instead of dwelling on my poor genetic inheritance, I try to rejoice in my rich spiritual one—resilience, persistence, courage. And instead of fretting over the stiff hands I awaken with each morning, I remind myself that I am still capable of touching many lives. ❧

🐋 Two Poems

by Carol Kanter

Telephone Connections

As a child back in Broken Bow
to feel less all-alone
she would climb on a chair
crank the phone above her head
and tell the Operator
to get her Dad.
I doubt anyone prompted her
to add Please.
For years our daily calls defied
300 miles and more,
part of her phone-a-thon that stretched
family and friends dawn-to-dark
to fill the hollow place
my father left,
to stave off her ancient terror
of the all-alone.

No longer will we talk each day.
I will not return home again
to find eight messages:
Call me right away.
No need to remind myself
how she cries Wolf.
My phone has all at once gone dead.
With a shock that smacks
of the all-alone. ❧

Rachel Waltuch Nussbaum, 1915–2005

Homing

A shower
for my daughter
pregnant with grand-
daughter number two.

Number one, not yet two,
will soon not know
what hit her.

But her mom, who taught
kindergarten for years,
managed roomfuls vibrating
with needs.

So, a shower.
I fly to Atlanta to attend.
A lovely weekend.

As always, hard to leave,
good to get home.
But in the cab
where I usually call

my mother to report
a timely—or late—arrival
it hits me:

no one awaits my news
no one has worried
if I am safe.
It is the first of the firsts. ❧

༄ The Unveiling

by Marcie Weiss-Good

August 2002

I'M NOT THE SAME PERSON I WAS before Dale entered my life. I'm not the ecstatically happy woman I was when Dale was healthy and we were making plans for the rest of our lives together. In an instant, with his diagnosis of advanced cancer, I went from girlfriend and lover to partner and caretaker. And in almost an instant, I went from spouse to widow. But I'm also not the raw, devastated person I was after he died.

My husband Dale's dedication and unveiling was this summer. As my two children and Dale's two children lifted the cloth covering his headstone, Rabbi Brant Rosen described the ceremony as the unwrapping of a bandage from a wound not yet healed. A wound that might never be completely healed, but a wound not as raw as a year ago. That pretty much describes my year.

As I think about how I made it through this year, I remember that after my dad died we made fun of my mom: There goes Grandma again, making conversation with the waitress or the cashier at Walgreen's. There she is still cooking holiday dinners when we'd be glad to take over. But now I find myself in similar circumstances. Aha—my mom was grieving and trying to fill the huge hole in her life. She needed something to make her feel alive again, and she was trying to reinvent old connections and make new ones. I did that, too. A web of connections had helped me through earlier losses, and I used it again.

These were my connections:

To Dale: Photos and memories and stories about him. It helps me when people mention his name, as I do often. Inscribing his name on the temple's memorial sculpture, and seeing it when I enter that sanctuary, helps me feel his presence in a place he so loved.

To my family: My children, who took care of me, showing a sensitivity and maturity well beyond their years. Our family expanded to include Dale's family, all of us trying to heal. I took my time setting the Rosh Hashanah table, savoring each of my grandmother's dishes, each of my mother's wine glasses, each soup spoon from Dale's set. Aha—a connection to people I cherish who are not physically at my table but are still with me.

To friends: My oldest friends who didn't stop calling me, even when I couldn't handle phone calls. Who bought me endless cups of coffee, and sent me cards and notes. Who tolerated my being at book group when I could no longer concentrate on newspaper headlines, let alone a novel. And some of my newest and dearest friends who were Dale's friends. I guess I am their connection to Dale, just as they are mine.

To my community: Neighbors, doctors, therapist, and my group of sisters who anchor me on Saturday mornings: When I have allowed myself to show my vulnerability, others have stepped in to provide comfort.

To other widows: When I felt no one could possibly understand what I was going through, when—long past shiva—I needed to tell my story one more time, I found a group of widows about my age. We meet for dinner monthly, laugh at things only other widows could laugh at, and shed understanding tears together. Aha—I'm not alone.

To work: While last year at this time I wondered how I would ever handle my job and considered asking if I could just collect my salary, for the most part I have been able to work, and the routine, stimulation, and collegial support have helped.

To projects: Using my hands has been essential in my healing—digging in the earth and caring for flowers. Lots of flowers. One quilt, two mosaics, and an elaborate bead project, completed on Dale's *yahrzeit*, have tapped my creative side and connected me to other women crafters. As I piece together bits of fabric, pottery shards, and tiny beads into works of art, I begin to repair my life and create a new one.

To the silence: I have allowed myself time and space to think about my loss and grieve. But also to remember better times and hold on to what's still good in my life. To reflect on my own strengths.

And last but not least, to the JRC community: Rituals of Judaism, especially around illness, death, and mourning, were familiar and comforting. From the *Refuah Shlemah* weekly prayers, to hospital visits by Brant and Anita and *minyan* members, the funeral service, shiva led by the rabbi, the cantor, my daughter, and JRC members, to *Yizkor* services after each holiday. Without realizing it, I've been gently guided to begin moving forward in a healthy way. I'm proud to belong to JRC, my community who rallied to drive Dale to Kellogg for treatments, pick up groceries and prescriptions, cook meals, and make adjustments to our house to accommodate his medical needs. Who visited when we needed company and understood when we needed to be alone. Who smiled and laughed and cried at our wedding, and smiled and laughed and cried at shiva less than two weeks later.

The week after yet another Jewish ritual—Dale's dedication—I had another "aha." While the dedication was difficult for me, when it was over I didn't want to let go of that day or the feeling of being surrounded by family and friends talking about and remembering Dale. The next Friday night, I found myself at Shabbat services, not my usual place to be. After we lit candles, Brant suggested we close our eyes, think about our week, put aside the "bad stuff" and hold on to what was meaningful. And now I often go to Shabbat services for that very reason—to rid myself of the week's difficulties and to hold on to good memories of Dale, a nice dinner with friends, a comforting phone call. And I know I can't do it alone.

I will always feel the loss of Dale, but there's been some joy in my life this past year, too, and I'm smiling and even laughing again. As one woman said during New York's 9/11 memorial service, "We shall grieve that they died but rejoice that they lived." ❧

❧ Moments in a Sad Season

by Lori Lippitz Chinitz

in memory of Charles Lippitz

A Thought is Born

I gave birth to a new thought today
It was many hours
and a day
and a night
and a day
in the borning

first, shock
then, pain

then, heaviness of heart
my insides in knots
the mind unbelieving

now it has come
and it lies in my arms
peaceful
hungry

when I wake, it is there
when I sleep, it is by my side

the thought
that you are dying ❧

A Dream: January

We are children
playing in a swimming pool
filled with bright blue water
and colorful toys.
I am splashing, laughing
in water and air
infused with light and fun.

We have to get out, dry off,
dress, pack, and stand by our cars.
We are high up a mountain road
at the end
of a long line of cars, all idling,
pointed downhill as
far as the eye can see.

Families stand
next to their vehicles:
a giant, still convoy.
Down farther,
cars and road and everything
fade into a gray pea soup
of impenetrable fog.

The sky has become overcast.
Down a little ways,
my parents putter around their car,
pulling out maps, organizing things.
Suddenly, a sharp wind blows
and sweeps up the leaves on the trees around us.
I hear someone saying
something about autumn coming,
or maybe that winter's on the way. ❧

Finale

No more meds
altered, augmented,
increased, suspended

No more long, languishing days,
weeks, ER visits and hospital stays

No more interventions,
doctor meetings,
live-in nurses,
vigils by the bed

No more chasing the cancer
that has stolen him
and cast him aside, abandoned
like a stripped-down vehicle
in a shadowed alleyway

No more watching disease
cannibalize him,
squeezing his will until
he is more drugs than Dad.

Days are not wildfires now
but waves, coming and going,
one like the next,
rushing and retreating
over his absence
and the simple elegance of death. ❧

Charles Lippitz with daughters Rikki and Lori, c. 1960

Shiva

Here is what I've learned:
See the death of a parent
as a life-stopping event
a meteor in the heartland.
Visit the stricken, feed,
Call,
Keep company,
Pay respects.
Do not just send a card.

During public mourning,
Expect only to begin to sense
the contours of absence
in the new landscape
and to realize that, in place of
the aging, pain-wracked patient,
your parent returns,
at all stages of your life,
reanimated,
iconic,
teasing and tickling you again. ❧

❧ "I Am Content"

by Robert Israelite

In memory of Sidney Israelite

MY GRANDPA TAUGHT ME A LOT OF things: how to play poker, how to fish, how to treat strangers as if they were friends that you had not met yet, and that a brandy at 4:00 is a fantastic way to start the evening.

The last time I really saw my Grandpa was on a Saturday in Palm Springs, California. It was a bright, sunny day with nothing to do but enjoy. Grandpa, my dad, my brothers Todd and Dan, and I started playing poker around 11:30 in the morning. The munchies came out soon after, and so did the brandy. We laughed and played for a long time out on the patio. By dinner we were all so comfy that we decided to order in Chinese and just sit around and talk. It was a day of such worth that my life is permanently richer for it.

The last time I talked with my Grandpa, we exchanged only a few words. He told me that he was going to be fine and that I did not need to worry. He always cared more about the people in his life than anything else; he was comforting me, rather than the other way around. He told me, "I am content." I think I will hear those words for a long time, reminding me that Grandpa was happy with his life— what he had accomplished and how he had added to the world. We told each other we loved each other and then said good-bye.

My grandfather passed away a few weeks later.

At 10:00 A.M. on Friday, the day of the funeral, I raced out of work to get on the road as quickly as possible. I had filled up the tank the night before, and I headed out onto I-90 for the two-and-a-half-hour drive to Chicago. About an hour later I hit traffic, a lot of traffic—the kind of traffic that makes people turn off their cars and walk around on the highway just to cool off. Frustrated and at a loss, I called my mom and dad to let them know that I would not make it in time for the service at JRC. I called the cemetery (hurray for cell phones) and discovered that I could get to the graveside service early. The cemetery was an hour west of Chicago, just off I-90. Good thinking, Grandpa.

I arrived at the cemetery an hour and a half before anyone else. It was quiet and cool; a rainstorm had just washed through. I found the grave, where everything was all set—some chairs, a tent, and a few trees to lean against. Nearby was the grave of my grandmother, who had passed away almost twenty years before. I sat and had a chance to catch up with her, to remember.

One of the groundskeepers came by and asked me about my grandfather, and I told him about his work.

He told me stories of the deer that drop by from time to time, as well as the hawks and fox that live in the cemetery.

I told him that my grandfather had always kept an open door for everyone he met, and that at 4:00 P.M. sharp every day it was cocktails at his place.

He told me of the mother who visits her daughter's grave every morning.

I told him about my grandfather's charm.

I asked if leaving stones on my grandmother's grave was all right.

"Stones are fine," he said. "People leave all sorts of things—golf balls, cigars, even peanut butter."

I laughed and began to heal. By the time the rest of my family arrived, I had found a place of love and laughter from which to say good-bye. ❧

⌇ Questions

by Jon Marshall

"DADDY, IS GRANDPA SCOOP BLIND?" my son Andrew asked.

My father's head slumped, and his eyes grew watery as they searched vainly for Andrew through the haze of his faded vision. The question hung like a storm cloud over my parents' family room, too heavy with emotional thunder to ignore. Could I reply without hurting Dad further while honestly answering my six-year-old's natural curiosity?

"Umm, yeah, Andrew, Grandpa Scoop's almost blind," I stumbled. "He can't see much. But he's very brave and he's not letting it stop him from going out and having fun. You know, he is going to the baseball game with us tomorrow."

Ah, the baseball game. I was dreading the baseball game. Normally the thought of a trip to the ballpark fills me with joy, embracing me with happy memories. Family legend claims that my immigrant great-grandmother learned English listening to the St. Louis Cardinals on the radio, and my dad still talks fondly of his days as a high-school pitcher more than sixty years ago. Mom says I saw a game in utero the day before I was born. When I was seven, my grandparents took me to a spring training game where I saw the great Ernie Banks, cruelly hooking me as a Cubs fan for life. During my adolescence, when I couldn't even discuss the weather with my parents without getting angry, Dad and I could still speak the language of balls and strikes.

Andrew Marshall with grandfather Jonathan "Scoop" Marshall, 2003

So when my parents bought tickets to a spring training game near their Arizona home, everyone was excited. Everyone except me. The thought of trying to shepherd my arthritic mom and my nearly blind dad in his electric wheelchair through the sold-out crowd while entertaining three restless sons was keeping me up at night. Even with the help of my wife Laurie, I wasn't sure if I could take care of Mom and Dad and three children under age nine at once.

When we arrived, my anxiety only grew. My parents' supposedly handicapped-accessible seats were near the left-field corner, far from the entrance. The rest of our seats were in the bleachers down the right-field line, at the opposite end of the ballpark. We asked if there was any way Mom's and Dad's seats could be moved so they wouldn't have to navigate the wheelchair so far, but the ushers just shook their heads.

Laurie took the boys to their seats while I tried to guide my parents through the mob. Dad inched forward in his wheelchair, terrified that someone he couldn't see would bang into him and knock him over. He stopped and flinched every time a food vendor, carousing college students, or even a small child brushed by him. At this rate we were going to be lucky to find our seats by the third inning, and I was already thinking of giving up and going home. But finally an usher took pity on us and squeezed Mom and Dad into seats by an aisle not far behind home plate.

I fetched them some hot dogs and lemonade and then took some food to Laurie and the kids. My eight-year-old son Justin, who had fallen madly in love with baseball the year before, was entranced, following every ball and strike. Zachary, three, snuggled with Laurie. Andrew settled down with a huge bag of peanuts and asked me questions about every aspect of the game: "Who's winning? Why is that man running? Why are they wearing numbers? What's an out?"

I began to answer but soon grew distracted. I glanced over to where my parents were sitting and could see Dad's red wheelchair sparkling in the sun. I worried that the heat was making them uncomfortable and that Dad's inability to see the players was frustrating them. But when Justin and I walked over to visit, Mom was giving Dad a play-by-play of the game. He smiled every time he heard the crack of the bat against the ball, his ancient San Francisco Giants hat shading his face.

I looked up and realized for the first time what a blessedly beautiful day it was, the sun warming a sky of pure blue. Justin started describing for Dad everything that was happening on the field. He told his grandfather about his favorite players, like Aramis Ramirez and Greg Maddux, while Dad told him about old-timers like Mel Ott and Carl Hubbell. Justin shared some of his cotton candy.

I returned to sit next to Laurie. As Zachary snoozed in my lap, ketchup from his hot dog ringing his round little-boy face, I blissfully watched the game, relaxed for the first time in days. Andrew kept asking questions, and I was happy to answer them all. ✺

Murray Kaplan and Elaine Strauss, 1989

 Glossary

All words and terms are Hebrew unless noted otherwise

aliyah literally: to ascend; the honor of being called to recite blessings for Torah reading or reading from the Torah during services. Also refers to immigrating to Israel

Amidah literally: standing; a central prayer in all services, silently recited while standing

balaboste, balabusteh (Yiddish) an efficient head of the household

Bar Mitzvah literally: son of the commandment. When a Jewish boy reaches the age of thirteen he becomes "Bar Mitzvah" and assumes adult religious responsibilities; often recognized during a service where the community celebrates his new role; **B'nai Mitzvah** (pl.). The analogous female ceremony is the **Bat Mitzvah, B'not Mitzvah** (pl.)

bentsch Gomel (Yiddish) to recite the Hebrew blessing for deliverance and good fortune, said after escaping danger or completing a journey

bima a raised platform in a synagogue sanctuary from which the service is led

brachot blessings; **bracha** (sing.)

brit or **bris** covenant; usually refers to circumcision of baby boys on the eighth day after birth; **brissim, britot** (pl.)

bubbe (Yiddish) grandmother; **bubbes** (pl.)

Chabad the Lubavitch Hasidim, very traditional Jews who emphasize study and community outreach; derived from *Chochma* (wisdom), *Bina* (understanding), and *Da'at* (knowledge)

challah braided egg bread baked especially for Shabbat and holidays

chametz literally: undergone fermentation or leavening; refers to leavened food, to be avoided during Passover

Chanukah (see *Hanukkah*)

charoset special dish, usually prepared with apples, nuts, and wine; eaten during the Passover Seder to symbolize the mortar mixed in Egypt

chazzan liturgical singer in synagogue; cantor

cholent (Yiddish) a stew which cooks throughout Shabbat. Various recipes exist, but the dish commonly includes potatoes, meat, beans, barley, and spices

Chumash five; the Five Books of Moses, or Torah scroll, in book form

chutzpah (Yiddish) shameless audacity

davening (Yiddish) praying; *davener* (one who prays)

Days of Awe (English) the ten days from Rosh Hashana to Yom Kippur; the High Holidays

dybbuk (Yiddish) a troubled spirit appearing in Jewish folklore

erev evening; the eve preceding Shabbat or a holiday

gefilte fish (Yiddish) ground fish, mixed with eggs, spices, and matzo meal; formed into balls or oval cakes and simmered in a fish stock

get (Yiddish) a religious bill of divorce

Goldeneh Medina (Yiddish) the golden land; America

goyishe punim (Yiddish) a gentile face

Haggadah literally: telling; the booklet used during a Passover Seder telling of the exodus from Egypt

Hanukkah, Chanukah eight-day festival marking victory of Maccabees, celebrated by lighting candles in Hanukkah menorah, also called a *Hanukkiah (Chanukiah)*

Haredi literally: trembling ones; an Orthodox group adhering to a very strict interpretation of Jewish law

Havdalah separation; ceremony marking end of Shabbat or holiday

High Holidays Rosh Hashanah and Yom Kippur. Also called: *Yamim Noraim,* or Days of Awe

Kaddish Aramaic prayer used in mourning and at other points in services

kallah a gathering for study and prayer; alternatively: bride

kashrut laws and customs of Jewish dietary laws; keeping kosher

kippah head covering; (Yiddish) *yarmulke*

klezmer (Yiddish) a type of traditional Jewish music from Eastern Europe

kugel (Yiddish) baked pudding or casserole containing noodles or potatoes, eggs, and seasonings

Lamed-Vavniks legendary thirty-six righteous people, said to be the pillars of the world

latke (Yiddish) potato pancake eaten during Hanukkah; *latkes* (pl.)

Lubavitch (see *Chabad*)

Ma'ariv evening services

matzo balls round balls of matzo meal and eggs for soup; also called *knaidlach* (Yiddish)

meshuggie (Yiddish) quirky or crazy

mikvah pool or body of water used for ritual immersion and purification during conversions and other occasions

Mincha afternoon services

minyan required prayer quorum of ten adult Jews; group that meets regularly for worship

mohel (Yiddish) one who performs ritual circumcision

nachas (Yiddish) pride and joy

Orthodox the branch of Judaism that most closely follows traditional practices and beliefs; other branches are Conservative, Reconstructionist, and Reform

oy, oy gevalt (Yiddish) expression of anguish, frustration, or worry

Purim Jewish holiday on which the Biblical book of *Esther* is read; the holiday celebrates the triumph of Mordecai and Esther over Haman's plot to massacre the Jews of Shushan

Refuah Shlemah literally: complete recovery; prayer for a swift and full recuperation from illness

Rosh Hashanah literally: head of the year; holiday beginning ten days of repentance with prayer and the blowing of the shofar

ruach spirit or wind; in a celebration, a lively, spirited quality

Seder literally: order; Passover dinner recalling the Exodus from Egypt through reading the *Haggadah* and observing numerous rituals

shabbasdik (Yiddish) in the spirit of the Jewish Sabbath

Shabbat weekly Jewish holiday observed from Friday evening until Saturday night; Sabbath

Shacharit morning services

Shehekhayanu blessing of gratitude for having reached a special moment *sheitel* (Yiddish) woman's traditional head covering

shiva literally: seven; formal seven-day mourning period following death of close relative

shofar ram's horn

shtetl (Yiddish) village or small Eastern European Jewish town where many Jews lived before World War II

shul (Yiddish) literally: school; synagogue

Simchat Torah literally: rejoicing with the Torah; festival falling at end of *Sukkot* celebrating completion and beginning of Torah cycle

sukkah temporary booth or hut constructed for holiday of *Sukkot* to recall the Jews' wandering in wilderness

tallit, tallis prayer shawl with ceremonial fringes on corners

tefillin phylacteries; two hard leather boxes containing parchments with Biblical verses, placed on arm and head with leather straps before weekday morning services

Torah literally: teaching; Five Books of Moses

Tu B'Shevat fifteenth day of Hebrew month of Shevat, marking the new year for trees

tzimmes (Yiddish) stew of vegetables or fruit; also, state of confusion

Ve'ahavta literally: you shall love; a section from the Torah, also part of liturgy.

yahrzeit (Yiddish) anniversary of loved one's death; traditionally, a candle is lighted to mark the day

yeshiva (Yiddish) school or seminary for study of traditional texts

Yizkor literally: remembrance; memorial prayer and service recited at certain holidays in honor of deceased relatives and martyrs

Yom Kippur Day of Atonement; one of the Days of Awe or High Holy Days, marked with penitential prayer and fasting

zaida (Yiddish) grandfather; also spelled *zaydeh* or *zayde*

◂ Order Form

To order copies of any JRC Press publications, copy this page and fill out the form below. Please make checks or money orders payable to JRC, and allow up to three weeks for delivery.

_____ *Is God Still a Cubs Fan?* (updated "2000" edition)

_____ *Pirkei Imahot: A Celebration of Our Mothers*

_____ *From Oy to Joy: Our Holidays Across the Years*

_____ *From There to Here: Points on the Circle of Life*

1–2 books: $14.95 *per book* plus $5.00 shipping & handling*
3–9 books: $13.50 *per book* plus $7.50 shipping & handling*
10–19 books: $12.00 *per book* plus $10.00 shipping & handling*
20–49 books: $10.50 *per book* plus $15.00 shipping & handling*
50+ books: $9.00 *per book* plus $20.00 shipping & handling*

$_____ Total including shipping and handling

Ship to:

Name: _____

Address: _____

_____

City: _____

State: _____ Zip Code: _____

Phone: _____ Email: _____

Comments: _____

_____

Mail your check and order form to:
JRC Press, c/o Jewish Reconstructionist Congregation
303 Dodge Avenue, Evanston, IL 60202-3252
847.328.7678 • fax 847.328.2298 • www.jrc-evanston.org

* Different titles may qualify for quantity discount, but all must be sent to a single address.
Special prices available for booksellers and Jewish organizations